THE
SEVEN
RULES
OF
SUCCESS

WAYNE
CORDEIRO

Regal

From Gospel Light
Ventura, California, U.S.A.

PUBLISHED BY REGAL BOOKS
FROM GOSPEL LIGHT
VENTURA, CALIFORNIA, U.S.A.
PRINTED IN THE U.S.A.

Regal Books is a ministry of Gospel Light, a Christian publisher dedicated to serving the local church. We believe God's vision for Gospel Light is to provide church leaders with biblical, user-friendly materials that will help them evangelize, disciple and minister to children, youth and families.

It is our prayer that this Regal book will help you discover biblical truth for your own life and help you meet the needs of others. May God richly bless you.

For a free catalog of resources from Regal Books/Gospel Light, please call your Christian supplier or contact us at 1-800-4-GOSPEL *or* www.regalbooks.com.

Library of Congress Cataloging-in-Publication Data
Cordeiro, Wayne.
  The seven rules of success / Wayne Cordeiro.
     p. cm.
  ISBN 0-8307-4294-8 (hardcover)
  1. Success—Religious aspects—Christianity. I. Title.
  BV4598.3.C69 2006
  248.4—dc22   2006021951

1   2   3   4   5   6   7   8   9   10   /   10   09   08   07   06

Rights for publishing this book in other languages are contracted by Gospel Light Worldwide, the international nonprofit ministry of Gospel Light. Gospel Light Worldwide also provides publishing and technical assistance to international publishers dedicated to producing Sunday School and Vacation Bible School curricula and books in the languages of the world. For additional information, visit www.gospellightworldwide.org; write to Gospel Light Worldwide, P.O. Box 3875, Ventura, CA 93006; or send an e-mail to info@gospellightworldwide.org.

CONTENTS

Acknowledgments 4

Introduction 6

Rule 1: Listen Well 9
Mary of Bethany: Learning to Listen

Rule 2: Be Content 33
King David: When Is Enough . . . Enough?

Rule 3: Live with Integrity 55
Nicodemus: Going Public

Rule 4: Avoid Self-Righteousness 73
Judas Iscariot: Fatal Choices

Rule 5: Choose to Forgive 93
Absalom: A Case of Unforgiveness

Rule 6: Stand by Your Convictions 115
Herod: Swayed by the Crowd

Rule 7: Maintain Healthy Relationships 137
Abigail: Appeasing the King

ACKNOWLEDGMENTS

The Seven Rules of Success was a team effort—without the contributions of many, what you hold in your hands would not have been possible.

Thank you to the vibrant, hand-to-the-plow church called New Hope Christian Fellowship in Hawaii. This family of churches is made up of individuals who savor His presence in every aspect of life, and who serve with a smile that starts in the heart.

We are a "homeless church" that has to set up—and then dismantle what we just set up—more than 200 times every year. I never cease to be amazed by a group of grace-soaked saints we affectionately call our "Levites"; these incredible volunteers remind me so much of Jesus. I dedicate this book to these committed men and women who have not only allowed their hearts to be pierced by the truths of God's call, but have also allowed their hearts to be squeezed until they bleed into every extremity . . . even when setup begins at 3 A.M.!

Thank you to Dawn O'Brien and her editing team, whose alchemy and wordsmithing can turn spills on burlap into masterpieces on silk.

Thank you also to our staff of willing-hearted servants in relentless pursuit of God's best. Committed to eternal fruit, they give tirelessly and then say "thank you" for allowing them the privilege to do so! I am ever humbled by their reckless abandon.

And to the many mentors in my life who constantly support my weary hands when they want to fall limp. You have selflessly overlooked my flaws and helped me to focus the light on the King and, by doing so, have helped me learn lessons when you could have disqualified me altogether!

And thank you to my wife, Anna, who has been my dearest friend for more than 32 years. If given the chance, I'd marry you all over again!

INTRODUCTION

*What does an outdated book containing names I can't
even pronounce have to do with me?*

Although you might not know it, the Bible is much
more than an archaic book of history. It is living testament designed to mentor us in our marriages, relationships and problems. It gives warning signs that alert us to
temptation. It can keep us from the pitfalls that have
destroyed others. It is not full of fiction; it is packed with
real people, people like you and me with a lot of character
. . . but not necessarily *good* character! We can learn so
much from them, both the good *and* the bad.

Take Herod for instance: His knees buckled under
peer pressure and he murdered someone he respected
. . . John the Baptist. Later, as if matters weren't bad
enough, Herod played a critical part in executing Jesus.
First, the messenger, and then the Messiah.

And there's King David, who took a "second look"
at a married woman in his neighborhood, and his life
was changed forever. Or Mary, sister to the original
Martha Stewart. Add a dissatisfied worker (Judas);
some sibling rivalry (Absalom); a fearful, questioning

Nicodemus; a woman (Abigail) who married a fool for a husband, and you've got your instructors for this short course in living.

> By faith Abel offered to God a better sacrifice than Cain, through which he obtained the testimony that he was righteous, God testifying about his gifts, and through faith, though he is dead, he still speaks (Heb. 11:4).

Although these biblical characters have died, their lessons have not. Their voices still speak, their scars have stories, and they can instruct us how to avoid violating the Rules of Success. These Veterans of Common Wars, with mistakes washed in tears and honed by time, can guide us new recruits to hopeful futures.

> Now these things happened to them as an example, and they were written for our instruction (1 Cor. 10:11).

Search through the fine pages of the Bible and you'll find so much more than old stories; you'll find life-changing gems that will impact your life, marriage and future. What you discover will influence the way you think. It will change your attitude and it will increase your ability to believe.

The path of the godly isn't always a straight line, but when you follow God's rules, you can be assured that the best is yet to come!

LISTEN WELL

MARY OF BETHANY: LEARNING TO LISTEN

---

*As Jesus and his disciples were on their way,
he came to a village where a woman named
Martha opened her home to him. She had a sister
called Mary, who sat at the Lord's feet
listening to what he said.*

LUKE 10:38-39, *NIV*

Millions of bits of information are relentlessly darting around you every moment of the day. An infinite array of waves are barraging and inundating you—radio waves, microwaves, television signals, cell phone frequencies, satellite transmissions—filling the very room you're in, bouncing off of you right now. You can neither hear nor see them, unless you are tuned in with the right device.

Frequencies of information carrying global content pass through us painlessly and undetected . . . *unless* we choose to notice them by tuning in. Thanks to the wonders of technology, with a radio or television set we are able to hear and see the digitally enhanced wonders of life—from cooking shows to the latest epic movies.

A GREATER FREQUENCY

There is another frequency that many people never pick up. It doesn't contain music or sitcoms. It carries the most life-changing information ever encountered. Filled with eternal direction and indispensable wisdom, these messages often go undetected.

They're highly personal messages that carry sensitive information about you, your future and your potential. These messages even warn you of unknown weaknesses and instruct you in people skills.

The Divine Announcer

"In the beginning was the Word, and the Word was with God, and the Word was God" (John 1:1).

God is speaking directly to us. He has been since the beginning of time, long before we were born. He is sending out signals—instructions and guidance—targeted just for you. He's sending you warnings of what is ahead in your life. He is delivering directions for your marriage, coaching you into your best future, and encouraging you through a season of despair.

The real question is not "Is God speaking?" Rather, it is "*Am I listening?*" His voice is all around us: speaking, warning, coaching, coaxing and correcting.

We live in a fast-paced, fast-forward world where busyness is equated with importance and success. In our society, hyperactively scurrying from one project to another communicates to others, "I am important!"

Carry a cell phone? You are normal. If you carry a cell phone, PDA *and* your cell phone is wirelessly attached to a Bluetooth device hanging on your ear, you must *really* be important!

But with all our "listening" devices, do we even know how to listen?

Only One Thing

A common malady today is ADD, what psychologists call Attention Deficit Disorder. This describes a person whose attention is short-termed and easily distracted. A similar phenomenon in Christian parlance is known as a *Spiritual* Attention Deficit Disorder . . . or SADD (Quite an acronym!) We're all prone to it. No one is immune from the SADD outbreak.

The only remedy is following the first Rule of Success: LISTEN. There is neither a pill we can take nor an antibiotic we can purchase; we must build it through discipline.

One person from whom we can learn the life lesson of listening is a woman named Mary, better known as one of two sisters, Mary and Martha. Through a snapshot of her life, we can learn how to sensitize our receptors to the eternal voice of our God.

Mary's story is one of the most beloved in the Bible. Mary and her sister, Martha, lived together, served together and spent most of their lives at each other's side. They were identical in almost every way except one: listening.

> Now as they were traveling along, [Jesus] entered
> a village; and a woman named Martha welcomed
> Him into her home. She had a sister called Mary,

who was *seated at the Lord's feet, listening to His word.* But Martha was distracted with all her preparations; and she came up to Him, and said, "Lord, do You not care that my sister has left me to do all the serving alone? Then tell her to help me." But the Lord answered and said to her, "Martha, Martha, you are worried and bothered about so many things; but *only one thing is necessary,* for Mary has chosen the good part, which shall not be taken away from her" (Luke 10:38-42, emphasis added).

Only *one thing* was necessary. Mary chose it (and so can you): to listen to the Lord. However, listening doesn't come automatically. It is a choice, a conscious decision.

Raising Leaders Who Listen

One of my favorite activities is teaching at Pacific Rim Bible College in Honolulu, Hawaii. We host, among others, many young high school graduates from all walks of life. Each student arrives bustling with energy and fresh dreams. You can hear them coming down the hallway to the classroom, their arrival preceded by peals of laughter punctuated with aimless chatter. But something happens to them when they settle into their respective chairs of higher learning. It might be the classroom atmosphere; once I suspected the air conditioning unit! Whatever the cause, when the lecture begins, movement decreases, eyes glaze over, thinking vanishes and they seem to pass into a state of "suspended education."

I remember one class session in which this phenomenon was taking place. I stopped in the middle of my lecture, called for a break, and had all the students sit up straight. In a loud command, I said to the students, "Wherever you are, *be there!*"

They gave out a nervous laugh, which in student-language means, "I think that was funny, but I don't know why."

I explained, "Each of you has the sole responsibility to present an awake, vibrant and energetic 'you' to each setting. No one can do that for you. Arriving and being present is not enough. We might as well fill the room with cadavers! You must bring your mind, your heart and your will to listen! If you are not here with the latter part of that equation, you will be marked *absent!*"

Are *You* Listening?

When was the last time you sat at God's feet to listen more than talk? You see, we need to hear more from Him than

He needs to hear from us! The way God created our anatomy is a great reminder to us that we should listen twice as much as we should talk, because He gave us two ears and only one mouth. But many times we get it backward. In fact, at the rate most of us communicate, we should have two mouths and only half an ear!

"Mary has *chosen* the good part, which shall not be taken away from her" (Luke 10:42, emphasis added). Listening is a choice we must make because it doesn't come naturally. We're too busy. I have to confess that too often, I identify with Martha more than I do with Mary. I tend to get too busy to listen. Are you like that too? I invite you to sit, just as Mary did, and learn indispensable wisdom. You may have heard the world give many formulas for success: "*The Five Secrets to Instant Success*" or "*One Fast Way to Save Time, Vol. II.*" But really, there's only *one* way to succeed. Mary found it. God commended it. Learning to listen to God is the first Rule of Success, and it is the only way to succeed in life!

It is the simple practice of learning to . . .

LISTEN

The only way to listen to Him is to tune in to His frequency. You see, God is clearly sending messages to you and me every second of the day. All we have to do is slow down, stop, be still and listen. Otherwise, like busy-bee Martha, He could be staring us in the face and we'd still miss Him!

> But the Lord answered and said to her, "Martha, Martha, you are worried and bothered about so many things; but only one thing is necessary, for Mary has chosen the good part, which shall not be taken away from her" (Luke 10:41-42).

Prayer is more than just talking to God, being "chatty" and busy with spiritual activity. Prayer is a two-way street where we talk to God *but we also listen to Him.*

A Two-Way Street

Listening is how we get to know the heart of our Father. Normally, we come to Him with our laundry list of items: "Bless me with . . . Change her . . . Change him . . . Give me a wife . . . Why did You give me a wife?!"

We complete our wish list, feeling smug that we've logged our requests with the Almighty. But we never get to know the *heart* of the Almighty! Because we really can't know someone until we listen to him or her.

Too often we pray neurotic prayers, thinking they're normal. But we don't even speak that way with other people! Why would we do so with the Almighty?

How would you respond if a friend called you and said, "Hi! How are you? Anyway, let me tell you what *my* day was like and let *me* tell you what *I* need. My wife is on the fritz again and my kids are all bananas. Yesterday I went to the gas station and can you believe the price of a gallon these days?! I can't! I checked my tires, got 'em all fixed up. Anyway, please be praying for my family; they really need to get their act together. Okay, I guess that's about it. Yeah, that's all. Thanks! Bye."

Before you can get a word in edgewise, he hangs up. When your wife asks, "Who was that?" you answer, "Oh, that's Roy."

Your wife continues. "Nice person?"

Your reply? "Yes, but he's weird . . . And I mean, really weird!"

We would *never* be so one-sided in a conversation with our friends, but all too often that's what we do with God. We think that the faster we pray the more spiritual we are. We pray but we never listen. And we never get to know God's heart.

Stanley: The Armchair QB

There's a classic story of Stanley, the armchair quarterback. It's the last quarter, the score is tied and Stanley is in the throes of the game. He yells to his wife, "Hey, Alice! Get me another beer. I can't leave this chair 'cause the score is tied right at the end here. Quick, get me another beer!"

She yells back from the kitchen, "Stanley, did you know a water pipe broke yesterday?"

"Just get me a beer," he shouts back.

"By the way," she adds, "it flooded the first floor, and our dog, Fluffy, was electrocuted."

"Hey, quit your chattering and just get me a beer," says Stanley, glued to the tube. "Oh no! Another touchdown!"

"Uh, Stanley, the vet said she'll be okay, but her hair will forever smell like burnt charcoal."

"Oh, for goodness' sakes!" yells the armchair quarterback. "Just give me that beer! And while you're at it, get me some chips, too."

"Well, Stanley, the plumber came and fixed it for $2,000. He said he was glad it broke because now he can afford to go on vacation."

"Alice, *what* is taking so long?"

Alice finally spills the beans: "Stanley, the plumber is leaving for Tahiti tomorrow and he asked me to go with him. Goodbye, Stanley. I'm leaving you."

"Alice!" Stanley yells. "What is taking you so long? You know what's wrong with this house? Nobody ever listens!"

What's really tragic is that Stanley's story happens again and again. We never get to know what's going on inside someone until we learn to listen. It's one of the indispensable rules in successful relationships.

Culture of Complaint

Robert Hughes, an art critic, wrote a penetrating book about American society, *Culture of Complaint: A Passionate Look into the Ailing Heart of America.* The thesis of the book is that we live in a society in which we feel entitled to all of our desires. Whatever we want, we should get. Whatever we want to do, we should be able to do. That's our birthright. When we don't get it, we give ourselves a "victim" status because we think that everybody owes us.

This culture of complaint influences our thinking, our faith, and our praying. Our prayers resemble marching orders to a genie in a lamp, making our every wish come true.

We're not listening for His will. We're too busy telling Him ours![1]

Be Still, My Heart!

Scripture says, "Be *still* and *know* that I am God" (Ps. 46:10, emphasis added). It's in being still that we know God. It's in listening and waiting for Him to speak that we begin to hear His heart.

Author Basil Pennington, in his book *A Place Apart*, used the metaphor of a still pond to symbolize our souls:

> When the pond is still and a stone is tossed into it, the effects of that stone entering the water with its ripples can be read over the entire surface. But when the pond is not still—when the water is already ruffled and tossed—the arrival of that stone will go unnoticed. Where the wind has already disturbed the surface, the stone will not be disturbing because it will be lost now in the frantic motion of the surface.[2]

God says, "I want what I say to be as a pebble dropping into a still pond. I want it to impact you and reverberate through your whole life!"

Listening may include our supplications and requests, but then it must settle into a posture where we train our hearts to listen by growing still. Stop talking and start hearing Him: "Lord, what are You saying to me about my marriage? What are You telling me about my heart? My attitude? My anger? My insecurity?"

In the stillness of God's presence, listening to His voice, I begin to understand . . . I begin to *know* His heart and will. Listening has saved me years of pain and unnecessary suffering. It has helped me to see people more clearly by shifting my personal vantage point from where I was standing to where *He is standing*!

Once you see the value of listening, wisdom begins to enter your heart. You can talk and talk and talk, but until you learn to listen, you won't know. Be still and know.

Listening and Growing

"Surely I have composed and quieted my soul; like a weaned child rests against his mother, my soul is like a weaned child within me" (Ps. 131:2).

God compares our soul to a quieted, weaned child. A weaned child is clearly different from an unweaned child. You've seen children not yet weaned from their mother: Each time the mother passes the child to someone else, the child gets impatient and throws a tantrum. As parents, we may feel loved because the child makes it obvious that he wants only us. However, we can't carry that child forever—he'll get too big for that! The child *has* to be weaned.

In his book *Love Beyond Reason*, John Ortberg explains this well:

> An unweaned child is a noisy child. The un-weaned child has learned that eventually noise leads to the satisfying of his desires. And even if it doesn't right away, the noise itself seems to bring him some type of relief. At least it makes others as miserable.
>
> The weaned child, on the other hand, has learned that the presence of his mother is more than just gaining immediate gratification. This child has become capable of stillness and can have a whole new communication with his mother because now the mother is more than simply someone who exists to satisfy his needs or take away his hunger . . . Weaning means learning to live in stillness with unfulfilled desires for a while, but it is a mark of maturity, isn't it?[3]

A weaned child experiences a new kind of freedom. It is a freedom from dependency as the main source of security, and a reliance on what others say for your value. You are released from making enduring mistakes of pain in fleeting moments of disgust.

In learning to still my heart, a weaning process takes place. God becomes more than just one who gratifies my desires. He becomes an important influence over my entire life. Choosing to listen is a mark of maturity. This is the first step in achieving this indispensable Rule of Success. Then you must also . . .

OBEY

The second prerequisite for having ears that hear and souls that are still is that when He speaks, we must *obey*.

In Hebrew, the word for "listen" includes the unspoken expectation to also *obey*. The Israelites understood the importance of listening *and* obeying simultaneously. With God, they're one and the same.

Listening = Hearing + Obeying
I grew up in a military home with a First Sergeant for a father. He disciplined us in true military fashion: He laid down the stripes and we saw the stars!

During my adolescent years, I became familiar with one oft-repeated phrase: "If you don't listen, I'll take out my belt!" My dad wasn't just telling me to *hear* his words. He was instructing me to *obey* his words!

But each of us has a tendency to drift into dullness, a blunting of our will to listen and obey. It happens unconsciously, and its encroachment gradually and surely takes over. Like rust on an unused bicycle, this dullness soon leaves us with something which is good for nothing except the dumpster. It happened in the desert with the Israelites whose ears became dull to God's voice. Perhaps hearing His commands became commonplace . . . whatever the reason, they lost the privilege of hearing Him.

Dullness is a natural tendency that you must intentionally resist. Maintain a vigilant heart to hear and obey.

Write It Down!

Every three months or so, I take the time to write down what I believe God is saying to me for this next season of my life. I record the areas that need improvement. I list the major goals I need to accomplish and I catalog what I feel God is asking me to prune. I get as specific as I can. I revisit this log weekly until I accomplish what I believe God is asking.

Remember: A life of faith is built on action; a life of fear is built on the avoidance of action.

Each of us must intentionally resist entropy, a slow, steady spiral of disorder and lack of purpose. Entropy will cause your life to drift into a random collection of activities and meaningless repetition, but listening and recording the directions and instructions you hear from God can reverse your propensity to live as a victim of life.

Writing down what you hear God say will help you develop keen ears to recognize His voice.

"Tuning In" to God

Some years ago, I compiled a collection of letters I had written to my children as they navigated their early years. I would sit and write a lesson to them so that later in life, they could read lessons of life, which I titled *Gems Along the Way*. In a letter to my daughter, Amy, I wrote:

Dear Amy,

We recently moved into our little house in Hilo. It's a peaceful neighborhood except for a frustrated dog who lives next door and is in love with his own bark. He starts his annoying tirade at 9:30 P.M. and continues non-stop 'til 5 in the morning. About the time I get up from a sleepless night is the same time he curls up and enjoys a morning slumber. I feel like sneaking up on his doghouse and barking until noon!

At first, I was so irritated that I began to think of ways to quietly and effectively put that creature out of his misery. But after hurling a few rocks wrapped in some angry words, my frustration ebbed enough to allow me to collect myself. As time slipped by, I began getting used to this demonic canine. After a few months, I hardly noticed him at all. I became numb to it. It's amazing what time will do when you ignore something.

On the other hand, your baby sister, Abby, is just a year old. She still cries at night, but even though she's been making noises at night since she was born, it has never become commonplace to your mother. She never gets used to it. Mom wakes up out of a deep sleep at Abby's first cry . . . well, most of the time! She can also pick out the sound of Abby's voice in a nursery full of screaming children. Your mother has never allowed Abby's cries to ever become commonplace; they move her to action every time.

I wonder if we've made God's voice more like a dog's bark than a baby's cry?

If I fight against His voice long enough, my ears eventually develop a dullness. But if I learn to respond to His voice each time He speaks, it will always be clear, fresh and distinct. I'll hear His voice in the night, in a crowd of people, in the middle of the world, or at 2 A.M. in the morning.

Amy, when God speaks, don't throw stones. Don't allow His voice to become commonplace. If you do, He'll keep talking, but you won't be able to hear Him anymore. So keep . . .

Listening and Obeying,

Dad

Jesus said in John 14:21, "He who has My commandments and keeps them is the one who loves Me; and he who loves Me will be loved by My Father, and I will love him and will disclose Myself to him."

God is saying that if you listen, truly listen, you will get to know God. He will disclose Himself to you. It's when we have His commands *and also keep them* that we show true love. When true love is in place, He is able to entrust us with more of His Kingdom treasures. It all starts with a heart that tunes in and instantly obeys the voice of God.

More Like Mike

When I was in Bible College, I was put in charge of our men's dormitory. Directly across the hall from my room was another student, Mike. He is a pastor now, but at that time, he was dangling somewhere between dubious and demented.

We would all play pranks on one another, but Mike fine-tuned it into a science.

It all started one day after school. He hid in the kitchen broom closet. As I passed innocently by with my books and homework, he drenched me with a 16-ounce tumbler of ice water.

I rose early the next morning. My goal was not revenge. Merely justice.

Coming back from the men's bathroom, Mike turned the corner in the dorm hallway and fell well within range of my water pistol. A perfect stream of water found its mark on his forehead, leaving me feeling like David must have felt when he overcame Goliath! When he regained his senses, I had already made it back to the safety of my room behind a locked door.

The final blow came later that night. I heard someone laughing outside my door, and I knew Mike had to be up to something evil. As I stood with my ear at the door, I could hear Mike's muffled cackling opposite from where

I stood. As I was trying to figure out his corrupt plan of revenge, I felt a strange sensation on my feet. Looking down, I noticed that not only were my socks wet, but also the whole carpet of my room was gradually being soaked. Mike had been pouring buckets of water under my door!

Livid with anger, I exploded. "You idiot!" We started scuffling and it broke out into a serious fight. It ended with Mike swearing at me, turning on his heels and angrily stomping off.

It took me three whole hours to clean up the mess. And with each torturous minute, I grew increasingly angry with Mike. It was nearly midnight when I finally fell into bed and pulled the covers over me.

"Oh, God," I said, "do something to that mutant! Burn his brain! Wait, he doesn't have a brain!" I lay there furious, plotting and praying, until I finally dropped off to sleep.

Wake-Up Call

Just after 1 A.M., I heard someone knocking at my door, "Uh . . . Wayne. Wayne, wake up!"

"Who is it?" I growled.

"It's me, Mike. I gotta talk to you."

"Get out of here, Mike. I don't want to talk to you. Go back to the padded cell where you belong!"

But he kept knocking.

This time I shouted at him, *"Why don't you just go to sleep?!"*

"I can't," came the wearied voice behind the door. "The Lord won't let me."

"Well, good for you!" I retorted.

He said, "The Lord told me that I needed to ask for your forgiveness. What I said was really bad and God won't let me go to sleep until I ask you to forgive me."

"Aw, man!" I said. "You're forgiven. Now get out of here and let me go back to sleep."

"Thanks, Wayne!" Mike said, "That won't happen again."

I pulled the covers over my head and complained to God: "That guy is such a bother! Why doesn't he just roll over and go to sleep?"

It was then that the Lord dropped an indispensable life lesson into my heart: "That's what you do, don't you, Wayne? When I talk to you. *You just roll over and go to sleep.* At least when I speak to Mike, he gets up and *listens.*"

There are times when truth doesn't seep into your heart. It explodes! And the shrapnel of that explosion left an indelible mark on me. I remember slipping to my knees on the still-damp carpet to pray what I think was the most difficult prayer I have ever prayed: "Oh, God, help me to be more like Mike."

This Season's Assignment

Take time to ask God, "How am I doing in my attitude? How am I doing in my relationship with my spouse? My children? My employer? My faith?" Then in your journal, write down what needs improving in this season of life for each of these areas.

Recently I wrote down how I needed to invest more time in my health, with my wife, and alone with God. Those three had been compromised. I needed to improve in these so I could fulfill this season's *assignment*. But that required hearing Him and then putting what He said into practice.

Hearing *and* obeying: These two components make up the definition of the word "listen."

And when we respond to God with a "Yes!" heart *and* a "Yes!" lifestyle, it not only pleases His heart, but we also begin to see His rewards.

SEE THE REWARDS

"Keep watching and praying that you may not enter into temptation; the spirit is willing, but the flesh is weak" (Matt. 26:41).

Prayer is a time to listen, a time to hear God's cautions and a time to make inner corrections that could save your future. Mother Teresa caught this. She was asked why she spent so many hours in prayer—was she listing the needs of her orphanage, or praying over the many requests she received from around the world? Her simple answer was, "No." Instead, she reported spending hours listening to God and waiting for His counsel so that she could move forward wisely.

Choosing the Good Life

Listening helps you to live wisely. It's a Rule of Success that will not allow God's words to pass by unheeded. He knows your future! He knows what's around the corner. He can guide you through the temptations that are lurking and (like Mike) waiting to startle you. Listening may save your family, your future, and even your faith. It is a most important rule of successful living, and the benefits are life-giving.

Notes

1. Robert Hughes, *Culture of Complaint: A Passionate Look into the Ailing Heart of America* (New York: Warner Books, 1994), n.p.
2. M. Basil Pennington, *A Place Apart* (Liguori, MO: Liguori Publications, 1998), n.p.
3. John Ortberg, *Love Beyond Reason* (Grand Rapids, MI: Zondervan, 2001), n.p.

BE CONTENT

KING DAVID:
WHEN IS ENOUGH. . .
ENOUGH?

Then Nathan said to David . . .
"This is what the LORD, the God of Israel, says:
'I anointed you king over Israel, and I delivered
you from the hand of Saul. I gave your master's
house to you, and your master's wives
into your arms. I gave you the house of Israel
and Judah. And if all this had been too little,
I would have given you even more.'"

2 SAMUEL 12:7-8, *NIV*

When is enough . . . enough? When will you have enough salary? When will you have enough house? How big is big enough? How many rooms will be enough rooms?

When will you have enough thrills? Adrenaline rushes? How close to death can you get and still have fun? How far can you push the envelope and survive?

Chasing after enough—it's a death-defying cycle, isn't it? And many never escape.

Especially in the case of money. The late multibillionaire Howard Hughes was once asked, "How much is enough?" His answer?

"Just a little bit more!"

How much is enough for you?

The answer to this one question reveals a lot about a person. It may surface hidden desires of greed, insecurity, or even anger. It exposes intimate information about the innermost chambers of the heart. Such a small question, yet it packs quite a punch!

Your "Enough" Answer?
When is enough, enough for you?

What would it take to make you content? A new dress? A new car? A new toy? More money, more time, more respect? Many of us, if we were honest, would answer, "Just a little bit more than what I have now, and *then* I'll be content."

Each of us is susceptible to a fast-spreading, undetectable cancer of the heart called the "Malady of More." This cancer-like growth is diagnosed by one consuming symptom: an unquenchable desire for more. Victims constantly grope for more than what they already have. And guess what? This disease strikes at any time.

How do I know? Because it's a natural inclination of the human heart . . . we *all* seem to want more. We desire more than what we already have. We can never be completely content.

The Malady of More is widespread and its victims are many. Individuals are both great and small: from schoolyard bullies to globe-trotting billionaires, from desperate housewives to dutiful ministers. This malady has no preference. It claims us one and all.

An indispensable life lesson, then, is to discover when enough is enough.

All-You-Can-Eat Torture

There's a restaurant in Waikiki that is an all-you-can-eat seafood and sushi buffet. When it first opened, the line of people vying to get in was ridiculous! Crowds would line the sidewalk all the way around the block.

They were often told, "The wait will be about an hour to an hour and a half." Many stuck it out, waiting for their chance at this "pie in the sky" event.

These faithful food hounds knew that for a nominal fee, they could eat and eat . . . and eat, stuffing themselves silly. We have a saying in Hawaii: "Don't just eat until you're full. Eat until you're *tired*!"

Well, once inside, the super-size-me consumer takes a plate (or two or three!) and piles it high. Some master the "Sky-High Technique": using carrot sticks as retaining walls! That way they can build higher and higher: crab legs, fried shrimp, shrimp tempura, filets of fish and sushi.

Then the stuffing begins. There's silence in the heavens for about half an hour as they gorge themselves with their stash. The silence is soon broken by groans of anguish, "*Oh* . . . I'm so uncomfortable! I am stuffed!"

"Well, stop eating!" you suggest.

"No way!" they retort. "I still have more on my plate!" They grab and gobble a few more shrimp. As they load and reload, the groans increase.

"*Ohhhh . . . I'm gonna split wide open!*" they complain, taking a few more bites of deep-fried shrimp and washing it down with a California roll.

This gnashing and grinding of teeth gives us a glimpse of the Bible's description of the place we're all trying to avoid! Have we stumbled on a parallel location to hell itself?

It's just another symptom of the Malady of More.

How much is enough?

"Just a little bit more!"

Every single one of us will come into contact with this malady at some point in our life. It happened to one of the greatest heroes of the Bible, one of my own personal favorites—King David. He was a great leader, superb general and a revered king, but David fell prey to the Malady of More.

Eye Spy

In the second book of Samuel, we find David on his rooftop porch overlooking the city of Jerusalem. It was a glorious city, the crown jewel of all Israel—containing both its capitol and religious center. After years of conquering neighboring enemies and threats to the children of God, David had selected this city as his fortress and home. David's long-term dreams included a son and heir to his dynasty who would one day construct a majestic temple to the Living God. Jerusalem would go down in history as the City of David—a place of peace and the apple of God's eye.

But on this particular day, David's humanity reigned. He stood atop his roof and surveyed all he had been given. Lo and behold! His eye landed on something he had *not* been given . . . a beautiful woman taking a bath on her rooftop. Now I'm not too sure what she was doing taking a bath on her rooftop, but the Scriptures tell us that "he noticed a woman of *unusual beauty*" (2 Sam. 11:2, *NLT*, emphasis added).

Calling one of his servants, he said, "Who's the girl next door?" And at the invitation of the great King David, this married woman came over for a visit. One thing led to another and they soon discovered that their one-night stand resulted in a positive pregnancy test.

Bathsheba's husband, Uriah, a leader in David's army, was away fighting on the foreign battlefield, so when the pregnancy became known, it would be obvious to everyone that Uriah couldn't have been the father. Eyes would turn in David's direction, because Bathsheba had been seen frequenting the palace.

To divert the rumors, David began devising a plan to make Uriah appear to be the father of the unborn child. Uriah was recalled from military duty for some R and R at home, but he refused to compromise his loyalty and integrity by sleeping with his wife. He chose to forego any privileges that the other soldiers were not afforded, and

David was left to face his own craving for *more*.

So David arranged a cover-up and had Uriah killed.

Your Gig Is Up

Enter the prophet Nathan, who recited a story for the king; hidden in this tale of greed was the truth that would help David come to grips with his craving for more:

There were two men in a city. One was extremely rich, and the other was poor. The rich man had many flocks of sheep. The poor man had nothing but a single, solitary lamb. Just one little lamb. He bought it and nourished it. It even grew up among his children and was treated as lovingly as a pet. The pet would come in and eat off the table and the kids would share their milk with it. Why, this little lamb would even fall asleep in the poor man's lap. It was as dear to his heart as a beloved child.

One day a guest came into town and stayed at the rich man's house. The rich man wanted to serve him lamb chops for dinner but was unwilling to take from his own sizable herds. So do you know what the rich man did? He went and took that one little lamb from the poor man and his family. He took their beloved little pet, killed it and sliced it up for dinner (paraphrased from 2 Sam. 12:1-4).

David's anger burned against the rich man. "As surely as the Lord lives, the man who has done this deserves to die! And he must make restitution for the lamb fourfold because he did this thing with no compassion" (vv. 5-6).

Nathan pointed at David. "*You* are that man!" David's ruse was up. God revealed it all.

Although he'd been caught in a web of temptation and sin, underneath, David's heart was pliable and willing. The prophet's words awakened him from his sleep of deception. Falling to his knees, he wept: "I am that man!"

When Is Enough . . . Enough?

David had many wives, conquered every enemy, ruled a united kingdom, lived in a palace and had wealth beyond measure. God gave him everything he desired. Yet David still faced the question: "When is enough, enough?"

We all have to answer that question when we're faced with the temptation of "just a little more." Is your "just a little more" in the area of finances, sex, possessions or relationships? Maybe "just a little more" means more influence, reputation or power.

Whatever our "little bit more" is, it keeps us desiring after what we *don't* have, clawing for it with our lives. The Malady of More robs us of the peace God makes available to us.

What is our best line of defense? How can we immunize our hearts so that we don't always desire a little more? There are three ingredients that will help to keep our hearts stalwart and strong. Let's take a look at each boost for our spiritual immune systems.

GRATEFULNESS

Each of us has heard a mother reprimanding a child who has just received a piece of candy. "What do you say?" she demands, her voice escalating. "What do you say?!"

Hurriedly, the child complies, "Thank you."

Showing appreciation is nice, even expected. But true gratefulness is more than token appreciation after receiving a gift. Another indispensable Rule of Success is developing a character of gratefulness.

Gratefulness is a spirit. It's different than acquiescing to a corrective parent and showing appreciation. Appreciation is a response *after* you receive something.

Gratefulness, on the other hand, is the state of your heart *before* anybody does anything for you. It includes thankfulness, but it's much more. It is developed through finding your security and satisfaction in Christ alone. In fact, the spirit of gratefulness is often developed in times of lack and poverty, where you find that God is enough.

I often say it this way: Sometimes you don't know that Jesus is all you need until Jesus is all you've got!

Grateful for Grace

Gratefulness is based on the root word "grace," as in God's amazing grace. This one word is so rich that the apostle Paul used it in every letter he wrote to open *and* close: "May God's grace be with you all." Paul understood the tremendous value of grace personally. In the original language, grace was related to favor, like a pardon or a free gift. This "favor" was usually undeserved and therefore something *for which we could never stop being thankful*. Grace captures the message of the Cross, the unmerited salvation of Jesus Christ. It is based not on what we want God to do. It is based on *what He has already done*.

So when Paul opened a letter or signed off, he was reminding his readers that the richest word for us as Christians is "grace"—the fullest source of joy.

Do You Value Grace?

Yet one of Paul's more pointed indictments against us was a failure to value grace:

> For even though they knew God, they did not honor Him as God, or give thanks; but they became futile in their speculations, and their foolish heart was darkened. Professing to be wise, they became fools (Rom. 1:21-22).

Paul understood that when people don't value grace and don't become grateful, they are led down the wrong road until their hearts are darkened. It's the right road to the wrong end! God warns us through the apostle Paul how very important it is to be grateful.

Have you ever been around ungrateful people? They live under the deception that they are entitled to "more!" The food is never prepared well. The traffic is never to their liking. The policies are inadequate and the leadership incompetent.

One of my favorite stories is about an ungrateful customer at a local restaurant. Calling the waiter over, he complained, "It's too hot in here! Turn the temperature down!"

"Why yes, sir!" the waiter cheerfully replied. "Right away!" and off he disappeared into the back room.

A few minutes later, the same irate customer yelled, "It's too cold! Change the temperature!"

"I will be happy to do that for you, sir!" the waiter cordially responded.

It wasn't more than ten minutes later, when the same customer raised his voice a third time, "Too hot again!"

The same waiter, with the patience of Job, cheerfully replied, "Right away, sir. At your service!" and again disappeared into the back room.

When finally the unappeasable customer left, another man called the waiter over and said, "That must be the most ungrateful man in the world! How could you be so polite to him? Why, I would have thrown him out long ago!"

The kind waiter smiled and said in lowered tones, "Oh, really, it's quite alright. You see, we don't even have air conditioning!"

A Joy That Refreshes

On the other hand, have you been around grateful people? Aren't they refreshing? They're the most rejuvenating people in the world because of their spirit. And that spirit of gratitude is positively contagious in making the world a much better place.

Joey was a baby when an accident left him with third-degree burns covering his entire body. By the time he was nine years old, he had gone through 70 skin grafts and surgeries, just because his skin couldn't grow with him as he grew.

When Joey was 14 years old, someone asked, "Don't you feel like you lost out on your youth? You spent most of it in the hospital."

His answer reflects a heart of gratefulness: "Oh no," he said with a smile. "I'm alive, aren't I? And to me, that's good enough!"

Gratefulness Means Enough

"Gratefulness" is a word for "enough." And when we begin to develop gratefulness, we'll find that our vocabulary will change. It's not "I *have* to . . . " anymore; it's "I *get* to . . . "

It's no longer "I *have* to go to church"; now it's "I *get* to go to church!"

"I don't *have* to serve; I *get* to serve."

"I don't *have* to take out the trash; I *get* to take out the trash."

Can you hear how gratefulness changes our whole outlook?

Gratefulness makes our lives special. It adds a sparkle to our lives—not a Pollyanna, pie-in-the-sky, false happiness, but a genuine joy that comes from viewing things God's way. And when we're faithful to deposit that treasure into our hearts, Paul says that we become wise. For it is then that we begin to understand when enough is enough.

That's the first gem to withdraw from this indispensable wisdom and deposit into our hearts: Understand when enough is enough. Practice gratefulness! The second immunization to protect our hearts from the Malady of More is this: righteousness.

RIGHTEOUSNESS

Righteousness is such an important element because it deals not with *what* you get, but *how* you get what you get. The Lord is *much* more concerned with how we get things. How do you go about fulfilling your deepest desires? Your wants? Your needs?

You see, the Lord is able to provide for our every need. Scripture says it this way: "A man can receive nothing unless it has been given him from heaven" (John 3:27). He gives us everything we need. But we can also scoot around the Lord and get it our own way.

Listen to what He said to David:

> I gave you your master's house. I gave the wives you have under your arms. I gave you the house of Israel and Judah. And if all this would have been too little, *I would have given you more*. Why have you despised the word of the Lord by doing evil? (2 Sam. 12:8-9, emphasis added).

David maneuvered around the Lord, even after He had gifted him with so much. The Lord still offered, "I would have given you more," but the way David unrighteously gained more for himself was far from God's plan for him.

Matthew 6:33 says, "But seek first His Kingdom and His righteousness; and all these things shall be added to you." What does that mean? It simply means this: If you seek Bible blessings, you've got to do it the Bible way. If you seek Him, seek also His righteousness. Then, and only then, will you gain everything the Lord has in store for you. Because when you do it His way, you won't have to deal with negative consequences.

Taking Care of (Private) Business

God understands that we all have appetites and needs. But how you fulfill those appetites and meet those needs is very important to Him. We have a need for companionship. So how do you get a companion? Through righteousness. Catch that because it's very important: The way to fulfill your needs and appetites is through righteousness. If you miss that, you'll compromise your faith.

That's what happens when a young lady sees a talented, good-looking man who has a lot of money. Too often she'll compromise her faith to gain that relationship. Or it happens when a man realizes he has a need for a relationship, but things aren't going well at home. So instead of asking the Lord, "How can I restore my marriage to what it once was?" he compromises his faith and goes for someone else. And the Lord says, "You're meeting your need, but not in righteousness." The Lord calls us to righteousness.

Consider the Source

We live in a health-conscious society. Everyone's checking the label to find out what ingredients a product contains, how many grams of fat are in it, and how many calories will I need to expend after I eat this thing? Let me suggest that we "check the label" not only with processed foods from the grocery store, but also with what we plan to get out of life!

What's the source? How is my need being met? Where is my fulfillment coming from? How will I get my needs met? Will it come from my own devices? Do I care? Will I receive it regardless of where it comes from or from whom it originates?

Will I receive it only from the hand of God?

Carefully consider the source.

If I said to you, "Here's a bottle of Evian water. The source? The Evian springs of France." You would readily accept it because it comes from a good source.

If I said, "Here is some filtered water from our nearby sewage processing plant," you would absolutely refuse: "No way! I know the source. I don't care how many times you filter it. I'm not drinking it!"

It's so obvious when we consider the source of our water supply, but we often can't see how important it is to check the source of our lives. It's incredibly important to consider the source, because the fact is, the devil can give you what you want. You can get rich without God. Millions do. Consider the devil's temptation to Jesus:

And the devil said to Him, "I will give you all of this domain and its glory; for it has been handed over to me, and I'll give it to whomever I wish.

Therefore, if you worship me it will be yours" (Luke 4:6-7).

The devil lets you know that he'll give you all of this domain and its glory *if* you compromise your faith. You can get your needs met in many ways, but if you choose to be righteous, you will be saved from any backlash in the future. One of my prayers has always been, "Lord, if it doesn't come from You, I'll have nothing to do with it."

Abraham Lincoln was a very eloquent man and a renowned communicator. Just before he got up to speak to the people to mobilize them, he would pray a shocking prayer: "Without God, I *must* fail."

What Abraham Lincoln realized, and what he was expressing so beautifully, was that he knew he could get up there and wow people. He didn't need God; he could do it on his own. We've seen many politicians—Hitler, Stalin, and others—do just that. But what Abraham Lincoln said was that without God, he *wanted* to fail. Even if he could wow the masses, he wanted God to make him fall on his face if he was without God's presence.

The book of Psalms says it this way: "I would rather be a gatekeeper in the house of my God than live the good life in the homes of the wicked" (84:10, *NLT*). In other words, "If it doesn't come from God, I'll have nothing to do with it. Even if it means I'll be a doorman for the rest of eternity." What a courageous prayer! Proverbs was written by the wisest man in the world at that time, Solomon. Listen to his words: "It is the blessings of the Lord that makes rich, and He adds no sorrow to it" (10:22).

Good source!

NEARNESS

What satisfies you? I mean, *really* satisfies you? Having more? For a Christian, it is not more. It is "near":

> How blessed is the one whom You choose and *bring near* to You, to dwell in Your courts. We will be *satisfied* with the goodness of Your house, Your holy temple (Ps. 65:4, emphasis added).

Psalm 65 is one of the most precious psalms. It's written by the same man who fell into sin with Bathsheba, the very one who murdered a friend to cover up his adultery, the one who pulled away from God's favor: David. After a season of repentance, he drew near to the Lord and was found to be a "man after God's own heart" (1 Sam. 13:14). A little late, but he realized that what really satisfied him was not companionship with another man's wife. It was nearness to God:

But as for me, *the nearness of God* is my good
(Ps. 73:28, emphasis added).

What David expressed was this: When you're near
God, everything which is not of God is not appealing,
because the Lord is your fill. For the one who wants to
follow God's ways, what satisfies is only one thing:
being near to God.

You can have millions of dollars, but if you're not
near to God, you won't be satisfied. You can be a CEO
of a successful company, but if you are not near to God,
your work will be dissatisfying. You can be an elder in a
church or even a pastor, but if you are not near to God,
the ministry will not satisfy.

Your Spiritual Timecard and Punching In

Some of us have a relationship with God that resembles
punching a spiritual timecard. You clock in regularly
on Sunday morning. You sing songs in church and hear
the sermon. You may even pray. But then you leave and
clock out, back to your regularly scheduled routine.
And you wonder, "Whatever happened to God in my
life?" Even Christianity can be a dissatisfying experience
if you do not draw near to Him.

Let David's words ring in your heart: "How blessed
is the one whom You choose to bring near to You!"

What satisfies? Only one thing: being near to God.

"Just to Be Close to You!"

Let me tell you a story about my youngest daughter, Abigail. When she was a toddler, she had the privilege of sleeping in our bed with Mom whenever I was traveling. But when I came home, she would be required to sleep in her own bed. She didn't mind Dad being away on trips because that meant she got to sleep in the "big bed" with Mom.

I returned from an extended trip to Japan and crawled into bed for some long-awaited rest. Within a few short minutes, a little girl was standing next to my bed. "What's going on, Abby?" I asked.

In the most innocent pleading voice, my child said, "Can I sleep with you and Mom in your bed?"

"No, Daddy's home now. Remember the deal? Now go on back to your own bed." With that I rolled back over, ready to drop into dreamland.

I was just about ready to enter the place between slumber and unconsciousness when I felt a presence. It was looming over me. I snapped to attention and was confronted by a wide-eyed daughter staring at me.

"Abby!" I said, "What are you doing?!"

"I wanna sleep here!" she insisted.

"No, Abby, go to your own bed. Dad paid good money for it, now use the thing!"

Undeterred, she continued, "Then can I sleep on the floor next to your bed?"

"You aren't sleeping on the floor; sleep on your bed!" And being the compassionate father I am, I marched her off to her bed, closed and locked my door behind me and drifted off to sleep.

I rose early the next morning, and when I unlocked the bedroom door, cuddled up on the opposite side of the closed door was the lump of a child. Half-covered by her baby blanket, she was lying on the cold tile floor, sound asleep. My heart melted. She had found her way to the closest possible point where she could be near to Mom and Dad. The hardness of the floor didn't matter, only that she was near us.

She was satisfied.

What satisfies you? If you'll drop nearness into your heart, along with righteousness and gratefulness, you'll boost your spiritual immune system against an outbreak of "just a little more." Then when someone asks, "When is enough, enough?" you'll be able to say, "*Right now*, because I'm near to Jesus!"

LIVE WITH INTEGRITY

NICODEMUS: GOING PUBLIC

Now there was a man of the Pharisees named Nicodemus, a member of the Jewish ruling council. He came to Jesus at night and said, "Rabbi, we know you are a teacher who has come from God. For no one could perform the miraculous signs you are doing if God were not with him."

JOHN 3:1-2, *NIV*

CAUTION: This indispensable Rule of Success comes with a bit of a curveball. If you're not prepared, you may be taken off guard. It's a good curveball, but a curveball nonetheless.

Uncovered or Undercover?

Ever hear of an undercover agent? One of the most popular characters ever created was one such character: James Bond. Don't recognize him by that name? Maybe I should introduce him as "Bond, James Bond." Or, "Agent Double-Oh Seven." As a mysterious undercover agent, 007 is able to foil the plans of even the most evil masterminds.

In real life, there actually are undercover agents who pose as spies to get information. Their mission? To uncover the truth while living a life of secrecy and deception. A little ironic, but that's exactly the name of their game: hiding their own identity while uncovering the truth about someone else. It's a dual life, a double identity.

The Curveball

And here's where the curveball comes. You see, there was an undercover agent in the Bible! A real-life, recorded-in-God's-Word secret spy who lived a life of espionage and deception. The third Rule of Success comes from this shady character, the "undercover disciple" named Nicodemus. The Rule?

Go public with your faith early on.

Nicodemus had the great honor of meeting and believing in Jesus. But he also had the great agony of struggling to go public with his faith. In essence, he became the secret "007" disciple—never able to publicly proclaim his faith—unrecognized by his own peers for who he really was.

"And You Are . . . ?"

The story is told of a woman who went in for a simple operation, but due to complications, died on the operating table. She appeared before St. Peter at the pearly gates and said, "Here I am. I guess I'm dead."

St. Peter looked through his lengthy list of registrants but couldn't locate her name. He replied, "I'm sorry, but your name isn't in here. I don't think you were supposed to die."

"But I'm dead!" she replied.

"Well, I can't find your name," St. Peter insisted. "I'll tell you what. You get to go back! You'll have 30 to 40 more years to live."

Suddenly, the woman found herself back on the operating table! Since she knew that she had another 30 or 40 years, she decided that while she was in the hospital she might as well get a tummy-tuck, a face-lift, a nose job and liposuction.

The operation went well and she was released from the hospital. She came out a dashing lady! But just as she crossed the street, she was hit by a speeding car.

When she appeared back at the pearly gates, St. Peter looked at her and asked, "What's your name?"

"I was just here!" she replied. "You told me that I had at least another 30 to 40 years to live! What went wrong?!"

"Ah," said St. Peter. "Sorry . . . we didn't recognize you!"

Will Heaven Recognize You?

The Bible highlights the fact that the "secret agent" in our story—Nicodemus—came to Jesus only under the cover of night. He wanted to ask Jesus a few questions but didn't dare be seen by anyone. He hid.

Nicodemus was a Pharisee and a respected teacher, and to be seen with Jesus would risk his high status and reputation. He was an undercover believer, a nighttime disciple: the original "Nic at Nite."

Undercover Agent Gives World-Famous Verse

It is in this conversation with the secretive disciple that the most famous Bible verse in the world is found. It's ironic that John 3:16 is the most quoted Scripture in the Bible, identified with Christian believers everywhere, yet it came from a secret rendezvous.

Here is that brief but life-changing conversation:

Now there was a man of the Pharisees, named Nicodemus, a ruler of the Jews; this man came to [Jesus] by night, and said to Him, "Rabbi, we know that You have come from God as a teacher; for no one can do these signs that You do unless God is with him" (John 3:1-2).

Jesus could hear the underlying question that troubled the heart of the secret agent, so He put off any further chitchat and went straight to the heart of the matter:

Truly, truly, I say to you, unless one is born again, he cannot see the kingdom of God (v. 3).

In other words, Jesus pointed right at Nicodemus and let him know that all of his Bible knowledge wasn't enough. It wasn't enough to just know about God, he had to be *personally* born again.

Nicodemus was now lost, more than ever. So he pressed Jesus: "How can these things be?" (v. 9). And the Lord answered with the most famous verse in the world:

For God so loved the world, that He gave His only begotten Son, that whoever believes in Him should not perish, but have eternal life . . . Now this is the judgment, that light [has] come into the world and men loved the darkness rather than the light; for their deeds were evil. For everyone who does evil hates the light, and does not come into the light, lest his deeds should be exposed. But he who practices [or lives] the truth comes to the light, that his deeds may be manifested as having been wrought in God (vv. 16,19-21).

Jesus was telling Nicodemus, "Don't be a nighttime disciple! Light has come into the world; walk in it!" (Well, that's my translation. Jesus said it a little more eloquently.)

Packed within this brief, yet amazing conversation is tremendous wisdom for successful living. Yes, it contains the world-famous Scripture. But dig deeper and you'll find more than that. You'll find that hidden in this secret transaction are clear dimensions for a Rule of Success that could revolutionize your destiny: how to become a full disciple of Christ.

GO BEYOND JUST KNOWING ABOUT GOD

If we're to be true disciples of Jesus Christ, we must go beyond simply knowing *about* God! You see, even the Pharisees knew God; some of them even knew Jesus personally. They spent their entire lives studying about God in the top schools, the Harvards or Yales of their day. They would compete to memorize hundreds upon hundreds of Mosaic laws, and upon graduation they were known as the elite legal minds. They knew it all!

But knowing *about* God is only a first step. You have got to go further! You must be born again.

In America today, 40 percent of our nation calls itself Christian, but that doesn't mean that nearly half of our population would call themselves full-fledged disciples. They might say, "I'm a Christian. I know enough about God, so don't take me to a church. I'm fine. Nobody likes a 'Jesus freak.'"

Interestingly enough, the book of James tells us that even the devil believes that God exists! There is not a devil in the universe that is an atheist! The devil knows a lot about God, but that's not enough. Knowing *about* God without really knowing God may just be our greatest curse in America. An indispensable Rule of Success is to live your faith out loud.

Blondin's Walk of Faith

During the nineteenth century, there was a great tightrope-walker named Blondin. One particularly great day, he stretched a cable across Niagara Falls, walked across it and walked back. As he slowly picked his path, more than 10,000 people began chanting his name: "Blondin! Blondin! Blondin!"

He finished the walk and was met by unabashed adoration of the raving crowd! They screamed and cheered for their new hero. He did it!

Stoked by the cheers of the crowd, he began his next great feat. He took some sandbags, placed them in a wheelbarrow, and then walked across the taut, thin line to the Canadian border. Again he slowly made his way back over the treacherous, raging falls with the heavy wheelbarrow still intact.

The crowd cheered even harder, "Blondin! Blondin! Blondin!"

He looked out across the crowd of admirers and asked, "How many of you believe that I can do that again?"

"We believe," they cheered. "We believe!"

"How many of you believe I can take this wheelbarrow back across?"

"We believe! We believe!"

"Then," he continued, "which one of you will get in and go across with me?"

Silence.

Not a single soul amidst the throng was willing to get into the wheelbarrow.[1]

Putting Your Weight on It

It's like this: I can know a chair can hold me, but until I sit down I don't *believe* it. I have to be able to believe, and that means really putting my weight on it. It's the moment that I relax my whole weight into that chair that I make a true statement about my beliefs. And that's what faith is: a moment-by-moment, day-to-day decision to rest our whole life in God's hands. That's faith. Anything else is just head knowledge and half-hearted claims.

That's what Jesus told Nicodemus: He could not enter the kingdom of God unless he completely entrusted his life, identity, future, safety, past—everything—to God. He had to willingly die to the old and become a new person. "Truly, truly, I say to you, unless one is born again he cannot see the kingdom of God" (John 3:1-21).

Like Nicodemus, you may be asking, "Wait a minute, what's this 'born again' thing?"

The Only Way In

Allow me to illustrate it this way: Let's say that the immigration laws completely change overnight and the only way you can become an American citizen is by being born here. For some that would be fine, but there would be a lot of people who would no longer be citizens. They might argue, "Hey, wait a minute. I was born in Japan but I want to be a citizen, too!"

"I'm sorry, if you weren't born here, you are no longer a citizen."

"What do you mean?" they would ask in desperation.

"Sorry. You must be born here on American soil."

Still they would argue for their citizenship: "But I'm already born! In fact, I'm old. I can't re-enter a womb and be born again!"

"Yes, that may be true . . . but that's the only way you can be a citizen. You must be born again."

"That's the only way?"

"It's the only way!" comes the firm reply.

Then, after a slight hesitation, the person in charge adds, "Well, there is another way that has been provided."

"Oh? What's that?"

"The One who owns the universe has made a way," explains the immigration officer.

"Great! Because to be born again is impossible!"

"Yes, with man that is impossible," agrees the officer, "but with God it's not."

The Road to Heaven Is a One-Way Street

Well, here's what God did: He provided a way. To be born again, you would actually have to die and come back to life in this nation, the kingdom of God. So God died and came back to life for you. If you've not been born in the Kingdom of heaven, which none of us have, what you'll have to do (you'll *have* to because there's only one way) is to entrust your life to Him. Why? Because He is the one who died and came back to life on your behalf.

Jesus is the only one with the ability to make you born again. That's it. So if you're going to be born again in Him, your life is no longer yours but His. You'll have to completely yield to Him. You have to die to be born again. And then you no longer live, but He lives in you.

Now it's His way of thinking, no longer your way of thinking. It's His heart, not your heart. His love, not your love. Everything about you becomes new in Christ.

You might ask, "If I become born again through Jesus, then I'll have His heart, His life, and His mind?" Yes, that will be the new, real you:

> Therefore, if anyone is in Christ, he is a new creation; the old has gone, the new has come! (2 Cor. 5:17, *NIV*)

> I have been crucified with Christ; and it is no longer I who live, but Christ lives in me; and the life which I now live in the flesh I live by faith in the Son of God, who loved me, and delivered Himself up for me (Gal. 2:20).

Living Anew

When we choose to die to self and become born again in Christ, we are completely new. It's kind of like that lady in the joke we used earlier who decided she had a second lease on life and got a new self: new nose, new face, new tummy, new . . . you get the picture. Except as a person who is new in Christ (not in body parts!), you *will* be recognized in heaven!

In fact, being born again is the only way you and I can make it in, because it's no longer our old, sinful selves who show up. We are now identified in Christ, and we have full admission into the kingdom of God.

Being born again means I'm no longer Wayne. Wayne died when he was 19 years old. That's when I became born again. It's not my heart, but Christ's heart within me. It's no longer my mind, but God's mind in me. I no longer have my own perspective, but His perspective.

Each of us who chooses to be born again gains a new lease on life. Part of that lease is our Creator continuing to create in us the new man or woman. This means parts of us have to be reset; like braces on crooked teeth, old ways don't magically or instantly straighten out. But by the power of Jesus being born in us, we are constantly being re-created.

That also means I have to keep dying to the old me and to my flesh. The only possible way I can enter the kingdom of God is by being born again *daily*. If I allow the old to come back and take control of my life, I'm not really entrusting my life to Him. And what I have become is a secret disciple, like Nicodemus.

Jesus has given you a new heart to live a new life. When you live that life—thinking with His mind, reaching out with His hands, loving with His heart—a confidence surges into your life! And there's a whole new buoyancy and radiance about you. In fact, the Lord says that when that happens you become the light of the world:

> Let your light shine before men in such a way that they may see your good works, and glorify your Father who is in heaven (Matt. 5:16).

REDUCING TEMPTATION

Go public with your faith. This isn't just some Christian charade, with people acting and looking Christian. It's people who are, in their very being, transformed.

And the earlier you go public, the less you will be tempted to join the ranks of the 007s. I often tell college students to make it known early on in the school year that you belong to God. It reduces temptation. If you appear neutral in order to be trendy, you'll be invited to places you don't need to go to. Hiding from your new identity will make you open game to the lures of temptation and the sway of the crowd.

I carry my Bible in public and have no problem wearing a shirt that identifies me as a Christian. Come to think of it, it has been decades since anyone has invited me to a beer bust or a spring fling! But I'm glad! I don't need the temptations and I would rather receive what I get from God's sources, not mine.

A story is told of a small boat captain on the border of a country known for drug cartels. One day, he made an appointment with the Drug Enforcement Administration to blow the whistle on some activities. He reported that for the past three years, couriers wanting him to transport drugs into the United States had approached him.

"Why didn't you report such activities three years ago?" the officer asked.

"Oh, when they first inquired, I wasn't tempted at all," he said. "It was simply out of the question."

The officer pressed further: "Why do you feel you have to report it now?"

The boat captain replied, "I knew it was time when they got too close to my price."

Going public keeps you honest and it could save you from making decisions that would steal your future.

Fast Cars and Healthy Accountability

One day after church, I was zipping home on the freeway. I was really hungry, so I stepped on it, knowing I had to get home before my kids wolfed everything down. Before I knew it, a policeman pulled up behind me and motioned for me to pull over. I thought, *Oh, no! What? I'm hungry!*

I pulled over and the policeman strode up to my window. I looked over at my passenger seat and there was my Bible. Oh no! So I threw a magazine over it just before the window finished rolling down. "Yes, sir?" I asked, as naïvely as Mary's little lamb.

He asked me that terrible question: "Do you know how fast you were going?"

"Not really," I said sheepishly.

He was unimpressed, "Well, you were way over the speed limit."

I was feeling very low at that point but still tried to hedge a little, "How fast?"

"Seventy-eight miles per hour," he replied. "That's well over the limit."

I was shocked, "Seventy-eight! Come on, maybe 68 but not 78!"

"I got you on my radar," says the officer, as cool as can be.

"Well, you better recalibrate your radar."

"No, it's right. Could I have your driver's license please?"

I finally submitted and gruffly said, "Here."

"Name?" he asked.

"Wayne Cordeiro."

"Your occupation?"

I thought, *That's it. He's got me.*

I mumbled, "Um . . . pastor."

He paused for a long moment, and then exclaimed, "You're Pastor Wayne Cordeiro? I can't believe this! I was just listening to you on the radio!"

We mess up don't we? But when we do, we hate it because that's not the real us. We have to keep shedding our old selves and have authentic hearts that say, "I'm sorry. I blew it. I really want to represent the Lord. Would you please forgive me?"

Live Out LOUD!

There's no greater way to live than to go public with your new identity. It's a necessary rule in becoming successful in life. Be a full-fledged disciple! You'll discover that a whole new confidence will flood your life. You become a new creation in Christ. And the blessings of God will converge on you because He'll make sure that you're living the life He created for you. There's no better way to live!

That's indispensable wisdom from Nicodemus, the 007 secret-agent disciple: Go public with your faith! And in that, God will be able to bless you beyond anything you have ever dreamed.

Soon you'll love what you have become. It will bring a new honesty, a fresh humility and a new sense of security. People will recognize it. And so will the devil.

But most important of all, so will heaven!

Note

1. Phil Campbell, "Believe It . . . Or Not?" Michelton Presbyterian Church Bible Teaching Resources. http://www.mpc.org.au/resources/resources/19990822.html (accessed June 2006).

AVOID SELF-RIGHTEOUSNESS

JUDAS ISCARIOT: FATAL CHOICES

Judas went to the chief priests and the officers of the temple guard and discussed with them how he might betray Jesus. They were delighted and agreed to give him money. He consented, and watched for an opportunity to hand Jesus over to them when no crowd was present.

LUKE 22:4-6, *NIV*

An Unlikely Teacher

We're going to hear from someone who seems like the most unlikely person in the Bible to preach anything. You know him well. He's one of the darkest characters in the Bible and his name is synonymous with ultimate betrayal: Judas Iscariot.

I think if Judas could live his life over again, he would do it differently, don't you? After seeing the catastrophic consequence of his decisions (resulting in the murder of a friend and his own suicide), I think he would *demand* that he do it differently.

And if he could speak, he would teach us an indispensable Rule of Success for a situation that each of us will encounter and must successfully navigate: dealing with what we perceive to be another person's faults.

Murder Mystery

The problem started when Judas saw something he didn't like in Jesus. It struck Judas so deeply that he began slandering Jesus' reputation and even plotting His murder. What started as a simple difference of opinion soon raged out of control, resulting in first-degree murder. The conviction that he was right and Jesus was wrong caused Judas to fall prey to an insidious disease that is invisible and often fatal, a disease whose victims never realize it . . . until it's far too late.

When I thought about the tragic turn of events that ended Judas's life, I said to myself: *Wait a minute! Judas wasn't an evil person. He was chosen by Jesus to be one of His 12 disciples. He couldn't have been so evil from the beginning! Where did he go wrong?*

The Plot Thickens

In searching for an answer, it might help to return to the scene of the crime. Let's go back to the point where everything took a decisive turn downward for Judas. This moment is revealed in Matthew 26, where Jesus and His disciples have an argument. It's the one portion of Scripture that clearly defines self-righteousness. It also reveals a key clue in the murder mystery:

> Now when Jesus was in Bethany, at the home of Simon the leper, a woman came to Him with an alabaster vial of very costly perfume (Matt. 26:6-7).

One translation of the Bible says the perfume was worth 300 *denarii*, equivalent to an entire year's wages. Today that would be worth anywhere from $30,000 to

$60,000. In those days, people stored this costly per-
fume in an alabaster vial as a savings account.

The Bible goes on to tell us that the woman emp-
tied the vial over Jesus' head while He reclined at the
table. And here comes our clue; look at the response of
the disciples:

> But the disciples were indignant when they saw
> this, and said, "Why this waste? For this per-
> fume might have been sold for a high price and
> the money given to the poor." But Jesus, aware
> of this, said to them, "Why do you bother the
> woman? For she has done a good deed to Me"
> (vv. 8-10).

The disciples convened a little gossip conference
and traded opinions. The indignant followers said,
"What a waste! We could've given that money to the
poor! That's more spiritual." Another one piped up, "I
disagree with the way Jesus is handling money. He's not
placing a high enough value on using it wisely!" Still
another said, "Neither do I!"

But Jesus heard them grumbling among themselves
and quickly quieted them. Their limited perspective of
the situation was right (she wasted the precious per-

fume), but "right" only if it were about economics. Jesus helped them see the bigger picture. This was about redemption!

Still, not everybody understood.

All Except One

When the disciples heard this, it quieted their arguments and convicted their hearts. They stood shamed and corrected. All except one. Here's where the plot takes a tragic turn; here's the decisive moment when one disciple refused to relent and repent. Instead, he chose his own self-righteousness.

> Then one of the twelve, named Judas Iscariot, went to the chief priests and said, "What are you willing to give me to betray Him to you?" And they weighed out thirty pieces of silver to him. From then on he began looking for a good opportunity to betray Jesus (Matt. 26:14-16).

After the "gossip gathering," 11 survived. They processed it, heard Jesus' corrections, and came through. All but one. For Judas, the argument was fatal. He now felt justified to go out and slander Jesus and betray Him.

He was self-righteous.

It's tough when you are wrong and have to be corrected. However, what is much more dangerous is when you *think you are right* and try to correct others! So convinced was Judas of his righteousness that it allowed him to justify his actions. Self-righteousness gives a false sense of authority. It gives permission to defame others. It "justifies" disrespect, which often goes hand in hand with speaking against a person in authority.

Holy War

When we think of a self-righteous person, we usually think of a snobby, arrogant skeptic. But that is not often the case. "Iscariots" also come in Christian wrappings and fill our churches. If we are unaware of these "Iscariots" in our midst, they can catch the best of us.

It happened to Paul the apostle. He was on trial for his faith and in the course of his testimony, the high priest Ananias ordered him to be struck. Look at Paul's response: "Then Paul said to him, 'God is going to strike you, you whitewashed wall!'" (Acts 23:3).

I like Paul!

But when a bystander confronted Paul by pointing out that the person was a high priest, Paul readily repented, "I was not aware, brethren, that he was high priest; for it is written, 'You shall not speak evil of a ruler of your people'" (Acts 23:5).

I respect Paul.

Even the apostle who authored much of the New Testament refused the entitlement of someone who was "right." He understood that doing so would mutate him into one who is self-righteous.

Justified by Jihad

You've heard of terrorists who feel justified to plant bombs that destroy innocent lives.

Do you ever wonder how they can possibly feel justified? Because of *jihad*. "Jihad" is an Islamic word meaning "holy war" or "crusade." Jihad is waged against infidels, people who don't believe in Islam. And because extreme Muslims have such a strict religion, jihad justifies a person to stop others at any cost.

If you are perceived to be against their religion, heritage, land or rights, Muslim extremists are justified to wage jihad. When that includes violence—blowing up a bus, plane or building—it is not only justified, it is holy.

We cringe, arguing, "That's terrible! We should give the stiffest penalties to such terrorists!" Although that's obvious, we're blind to the jihad that we ourselves are waging. You see, we all share the same tendency.

Our Own Jihad

When we think someone is doing wrong, we've judged that person. Once we pass judgment, we give ourselves permission to take action. The underlying motivation is, "I can't kill you physically, so I'll do it civilly: I'll kill your reputation. My judgment justifies obliterating your name. I'll also cut my relationship with you and do my best to do that in your relationships with others."

We embark on our own jihad. Sure, we may cringe when it happens in the world, but it is perfectly acceptable when it happens in our churches and in our families. We kill each other, except we do it in the name of "righteousness."

Sounds holy, doesn't it?

We need to learn the indispensable wisdom of how to defeat self-righteousness. It is invisible and deadly, able to destroy not just individuals, but families, friendships, ministries, entire churches and communities.

THE LIGHTNING ROD

So what do we do when we have these feelings? Here's another Rule of Success that leads to success: Find yourself someone who will act as a faithful "lightning rod."

In the Midwest, electrical storms are common and lightning strikes often. Because lightning strikes the tallest point in the area, typically you'll see a rod protruding from the roof of taller buildings. This rod is grounded so that when lightning hits, it conducts the thousands of volts of electricity down into the ground, neutralizing it. Without a grounded lightning rod, the massive jolt of electricity would spike the electronic equipment and fry computer circuit boards.

We need people in our lives who can serve as living lightning rods. When I'm upset and I want to verbally attack someone, I instead turn to my lightning rod, laying out the issue as I see it. My lightning rod listens to me and grounds any destructive current. He helps to neutralize my anger so that I don't fry people.

Lightning rods listen and understand. They allow you to vent, and then they accompany you on a journey back to Jesus. They may recognize some validity to your perspective, but they won't let you fry people with your excess emotional baggage.

Lightning rods are not "yes" people. They don't have a deep need to be accepted by you. If they did have that need, they would end up shouldering your offenses rather than resolving them.

Danger: Shouldering Others' Offenses

It is dangerous to shoulder another's offense. Why? Because if someone is wounded, God's grace is sufficient *for them*. God gives that person ample supplies of His grace to allow that person to heal. His grace is always readily available for a wound or an offense.

However, His grace is not available for those who shoulder another's offense, no matter how loyal it may seem. Grace is available to the offended, not to the one who picks up another person's offense.

Carrying someone else's offense is like a flesh-eating disease—it'll eat you alive! It seems like a characteristic of a true friend, but it will only devastate you and everyone around you.

On the other hand, a lightning rod helps you to shoulder your burden in a way that leads you back to the Burden Bearer. Then only the unhealthy parts of relationships are pruned, and all parties involved come out on top!

THE BEST LIGHTNING RODS

When it comes to selecting a lightning rod, my rule of thumb is brothers with brothers, and sisters with sisters. Setting this healthy boundary helps you to prevent any crossing of wires *before* things get out of hand. Help yourself stay out of trouble: Set clear boundaries ahead of time.

A second consideration is to know what kind of person you want to become. Do you want to be wise? Slow to anger? Known for your understanding? Then those are the kinds of people you want to befriend. Those qualities, when seen in others, will produce some of the best lightning rods and the longest-lasting friendships.

There are three qualities I am always on the lookout for in others. They're ones I want to develop in my own life, and there's no better way than to hang around those who exude these qualities!

1. A Heart of Integrity

In this case, integrity can be defined as "protecting the reputation of those not present in order to gain the trust of those who are." When I disagree with someone who is not present, it's easy to speak bluntly and sometimes inappropriately. Carry that to the extreme, and gossiping and badmouthing others is just a breath away.

Integrity says, "Hold on! It is not for me to ruin that person's reputation. It's not right until I fully understand his side of the story." Why? Because the Bible says, "He who gives an answer before he [fully understands], it is folly and shame to him" (Prov. 18:13).

Do some research and allow the other person to share his side of the story. For me to come to a conclusion about his reputation, his heart, his spirit, his motives, without fully investigating all of the facts would be wrong. Doing so would reveal a lack of integrity. But as I honor that person by finding out the facts, I also honor God and I become a person of integrity.

When you have integrity, those in your presence will say, "You're right. I want to be like that, too!" If I slaughter someone's reputation when he's not there to defend himself, then those listening think, *Whoa! If he can slander that guy when he's not around, then what does he say about me?!* However, when I protect the reputation of someone who isn't present, I gain the trust of those who are present.

The test of integrity is one we'll all encounter at some point in our lives, guaranteed. So be prepared by knowing how to best respond—by refraining from snap judgments or unfounded gossip.

The second test of the heart I look for in my lightning rods is another tough one:

2. A Heart of Purity

Our hearts need to constantly be run through a purifying filter. Too often, they get clogged with humanity's excesses, and the resulting buildup taints our motives. Through no direct fault of our own, we become bitter, cynical, dark, even prone to sin.

I love to be around those whose hearts have been cleansed again and again, people for whom "repentance" isn't a bad word, and confession doesn't come hard. Their outlook stays just like Jesus': heavenly!

I want to be like that, too!

But typically when a situation upsets me, my negative reaction is the result of something impure already residing deep in my heart. It's usually a buried personal issue that I haven't resolved. Something triggers it and it flares up, irritating me and clouding my judgment.

It happened to Judas. He defended his self-righteousness: "For this perfume might have been sold for a high price and the money given to the poor" (Matt. 26:9). He didn't say this because he was concerned about the poor, but because he was a thief; he pilfered from the very moneybox he was in charge of running! What he was really saying was this: "Let's sell the perfume and give me the money. I'll hold it under the illusion of giving it to the poor. First, let me take my commission." His greed caused his indignation to flare up.

For from within, out of the heart of men, pro-
ceed the evil thoughts, fornications, thefts,
murders, adulteries, deeds of coveting and
wickedness, as well as deceit, sensuality, envy,
slander, pride and foolishness (Mark 7:21-22).

My Judas moment happened to me years ago when
I was at a retirement party for another pastor. He had
been in ministry for 40 years. To honor him, an offering
collected from all the pastors and churches in our dis-
trict was presented as a gift.

They announced the grand total, "We're happy to
bless our dear retiring brother with this gift of $40,000!"
Everyone applauded. I was clapping too, but on the
inside I said, *Forty-thousand dollars? This guy already has a
house and car, why does he need $40,000? Do you know how
much ministry I could do with that money? I don't even earn
that much! In fact, I won't earn that after working for the next
three years! This is so unspiritual!*

The applause died down and I heard the Lord call
me, "Hey, Iscariot!"

I looked around, "What, me?"

"Yes, you, Wayne," He gently scolded. I realized what
the Lord was saying and what had happened within me.
Greed had surfaced; that's why I was indignant: "We

could have taken that money and given it to the poor."

Get real! I just wanted it for myself.

When I'm indignant about an event or action, it's often because something unhealthy inside of me is surfacing. But often, instead of acknowledging the root cause, I blame the other person as the culprit and launch attacks of self-righteousness. Meanwhile, I completely miss the real problem: me.

God uses difficulties to uncover personal issues we haven't dealt with in years. We've refused to resolve them and now it's time. If we don't do it now, we'll continue to hit a ceiling in our growth with the Lord. Why? Simply because we're too quick to be indignant with others when really the problem is right within our own souls.

It can be the hardest thing to see that the problem is actually you. It's easy to point at others, identifying them as the problem. It's kind of like people with bad body odor. They can't smell it, but everyone else can.

The third test of the heart is just as challenging, yet completely vital:

3. The Heart of a Reformer

There is a major difference between a reformer and a rebel. They may look similar at first, but they end up at opposite poles.

A rebel is someone who sees a problem and uses it as justification and ammunition and for talking about others, even slandering and sabotaging. A rebel is a problem-finder; a reformer is a problem-solver. A rebel is not satisfied even though the problem is resolved; a reformer rejoices when there is resolution. The rebel's heart is fixated on the problem, whereas the reformer's heart is focused on the solution and hurries toward God's best for everyone involved.

Becoming a rebel is an automatic default in each of us. Becoming a reformer requires discipline and character. I chose the latter, and my quest for friends of the same fabric continues.

As I made that choice, the Lord showed me why He chose Daniel—because he had a different spirit, one of a reformer rather than a rebel: "This was because an extraordinary spirit, knowledge and insight, interpretation of dreams, explanation of enigmas and solving of difficult problems were found in this Daniel" (Dan. 5:12). Daniel chose to solve problems, and that set him apart, ready to be used mightily by the Lord. Choose to be like Daniel, a reformer ready for God to use in great ways. It's one of the best ways to become great in His kingdom!

These three qualities of the heart are important in locating lightning rods in life. They are, in fact, critical!

These friends will help you to find your place in the kingdom of God.

CHOOSE YOUR ROLE IN THE KINGDOM OF GOD

Many roles abound in the kingdom of God and you get to choose what role you will play through your life.

Through a series of unfortunate decisions, Judas chose one of the darkest roles in the Kingdom. The Bible lamented the person who would choose that role:

> For the Son of Man is to go just as it is written of Him; but *woe to that man by whom the Son of Man is betrayed!* (Mark 14:21, emphasis added).

The plan of God from the beginning of time was for the Messiah to come, to be betrayed and to die on the cross. This plan included someone who would betray Him. But who it would be wasn't predetermined. There were many roles available in the unfolding drama: Some would follow, some would run, some would support Him, some would care for His body, some would pray, and some would insidiously plot His death.

By the way, which of these roles will you play?

You get to choose. If you choose to be great in the kingdom of God, you will be great. If you choose to be a neutral part of the Kingdom, you will be neutral. Choose to be a spectator and that's what you'll be. Choose to be one who walks through life kicking stones and life will be a hard road for you. "According to your faith, it shall be done unto you" (Matt. 9:29, *NIV*).

You Are the Company You Keep

A while ago I went to Denver to watch their Major League Baseball team, the Colorado Rockies, play the Dodgers at Coors Stadium. I knew one of the pitchers for the Dodgers. He had grown up in Hilo, and he and his family were members of our church.

I sat down smack-dab in the middle of about 20,000 Rockies fans in Coors Stadium. I was engulfed in a sea of purple, the Rockies' team color. It seemed like the whole stadium was cheering for the "wrong" team, as my humble Dodgers were obviously outnumbered. Whenever the Rockies got a good hit, it sounded like the entire state was roaring its approval. Amidst the deafening Rockies fans, I would attempt a pitiful little yell, "No!" but you couldn't hear me in the roar of 20,000 purple fanatics. This David versus Goliath competition continued for the first few innings as I was literally overwhelmed by purple pride.

After a while I started talking with these enthusiastic Rockies fans and caught their excitement. When the Rockies had a good hit, they would all stand up and yell, "Yay! Good hit!"

And I would nod, "Yeah, that *was* a pretty good hit."

It was in the fourth inning when their contagious enthusiasm completely overtook me; I switched teams. So much for my pitcher friend. I was a turncoat and when the Rockies won, I swelled with purple pride!

A Not-So-Happy Ending

Choose wisely who you will allow to influence your life, because you become the company you keep. It's another vital Rule of Success that can launch you to success or dash your destiny. Choose life!

Lightning rods become lifelong friends. They warn you of impending harm and the slow overgrowth of self-righteousness. They help you become the person you've always wanted to be, and they save you from your own humanity.

I wish Judas had a lightning rod.

It could have saved him 30 pieces of silver.

CHOOSE TO FORGIVE

ABSALOM:
A CASE OF UNFORGIVENESS

*Her brother Absalom said to her, "Has that
Amnon, your brother, been with you? Be quiet now,
my sister; he is your brother." Absalom never said a
word to Amnon, either good or bad; he hated Amnon
because he had disgraced his sister Tamar.*

2 SAMUEL 13:20,22, *NIV*

The fifth Rule of Success is also one of the toughest.

The greatest gift our hearts will ever know is the gift of forgiveness. When we learn this, we'll have caught the heart of a loving God. And in learning it, we'll be able to extend it to others.

Ironically, we're about to learn forgiveness from someone who was unforgiving. In fact, this person was unforgiving because others were unforgiving to him!

This pillar of unforgiveness is one of David's sons, Absalom.

Grab a box of Kleenex; we're going to watch a soap opera. Today's story has it all: a lusting prince, a deceived woman, a palace murder, jealousy, intrigue and scandal . . . complete with a cliff-hanger ending! (Men: Hang on, there's a sub-woofer-pulsating battle scene at the end of the episode.)

Allow me to unfold Absalom's captivating story.

SCENE 1: ALL MY CHILDREN

King David had many sons, the best known of whom was Solomon. Another brother, Absalom, was renowned as a great warrior. Absalom's sister, Tamar, was famous for her beauty.

On another side of King David's court lived a half-brother, Amnon.

As time passed, Amnon became obsessed by his half-sister Tamar, until his lustful obsession grew out of control. One fateful day, Amnon tricked Tamar into entering his private tent and there he raped her. But the tragedy didn't end there. It never does. With his lust satisfied, Amnon's "love" turned to disgust, and Tamar was thrown out into the street. In those days, a raped woman was a defiled woman, doomed to never marry, forced to a future of shame and prostitution.

Tamar's brother Absalom discovered his sister's exploitation. Incensed at the injustice, Absalom stowed his revenge in the deep chambers of his heart, murmuring, "Be patient, sister. I'll take care of everything."

For two years, Absalom quietly held it all inside. But his resentment, like radioactive waste, contaminated his relationships and mutated his personality. He began to morph into the very one he despised. And, as you'll see, his decisions were about to ruin his destiny.

Revenge: A Dish Best Served Cold

The day of reckoning finally arrived. The royal family gathered during the time of the sheep-shearing festival, and it was the perfect cover for murder.

Absalom stroked a lock of his hair. "Amnon, I want to invite you to our family party."

Amnon was relieved. *At last!* he thought, *I'm back in with my big brother!* And like a fox lured to a baited trap, Amnon accepted the invitation and went to the party.

Absalom invited Amnon for a private stroll, and as they rounded a corner, Absalom pulled a knife and slid it into his brother's heart.

The rest of the party fled, and soon the news of Absalom's murderous revenge reached the ears of his father, King David. David realized that Absalom had to die or be banished.

Banished!

"Absalom, you must leave our city of Jerusalem!"

"What do you mean, 'leave the city'?!" cried Absalom. "Amnon was the one who was wrong!" With quiet restraint King David wisely answered, "You need to forgive."

"Forgive *him*?" Absalom interrupted. "Don't you realize there was an injustice? You can't downplay what happened!"

Already the story of Absalom is rife with sex, revenge and scandal in the highest offices of the land. The royal family was in an uproar and the number of life lessons we can learn are as many as the subplots. But above all, Absalom's self-righteous indignation reflected a heart that didn't understand forgiveness.

Before we make the same mistake, let's get clear on what forgiveness is . . . and is not.

Three things forgiveness is *not*:

1. **Forgiveness does *not* mean an injustice has not taken place.** The need for forgiveness is usually because an injustice has indeed taken place. Although a wrong has been experienced, be careful not to enter into an even greater wrong by holding on to it. That easily turns injustice into tragedy. Forgiveness is not dismissing an injustice; it's being freed from it so that *you* can move on.

2. **Forgiveness does *not* mean you are passive or soft about sin.** God forgives freely, but remember, that cost Him everything! There was nothing soft (or easy) about it! When we follow His example, we learn that forgiveness isn't being soft on sin; it's being righteous through it. Which leads us directly to the final thing that forgiveness is not . . .

3. **Forgiveness does *not* mean you have to compromise righteousness.** You are not a less righteous person because you forgive. In fact, it is one of the greatest indicators of righteousness! Forgiveness has nothing to do with compromising righteousness; instead, it has everything to do with increasing in it!

Scene 2: As the Stomach Churns

With these parameters clearly set about what forgiveness is *not*, let's continue the saga of Absalom. He was banished to the equivalent of Siberia. One might think living there would cool his anger—we've heard time heals all wounds—but unresolved anger doesn't cool with time. It burns bitterly like a deep ulcer.

Another common misconception is that revenge quenches anger. It doesn't. In fact, Absalom's bitterness was not washed clean with Amnon's blood . . . it whetted his appetite for more.

Three years later, Absalom was readmitted to Jerusalem, but his relationship with his father remained distant. For two more years, they neither saw nor spoke to one another. Absalom's anger resurfaced: "How dare my father not acknowledge me! I am a prince after all and this is the royal city!"

Enlisting one of David's generals, he put out his orders: "Get my father to call me and embrace me in public. I need to be accepted again by my father, the king, and publicly restored to my rightful place as prince."

David still refused.

Enraged, Absalom set fire to the general's wheat field, thinking, *I'll get a response now!* The general came rushing and demanded, "What in the world are you doing?"

"I wanted your attention," said Absalom. "I wanted an audience but you wouldn't get it for me. So I burned your field."

The lack of forgiveness makes you desperate. It leads to poor decision-making, a disrespect that seems justified, and blindness to everything foolish. Ultimately, it spawns a warped character, which is exactly what Absalom had become.

"If *I* Were King . . ."

David finally gave in to Absalom's tantrums, formally receiving him back to Jerusalem. Did that satisfy Absalom? No. Unforgiveness refuses to be satisfied.

Instead of repenting, he began to resent his father and started a campaign to become king himself. Anytime he came across a complaining citizen in his father's empire, Absalom would assure that person, "If I were the king, I would help you."

Eventually, Absalom succeeded in turning the hearts of the people away from King David. His case seemed so just and his willingness to improve matters sounded selflessly noble, but Absalom's motives were corrupt and his heart hardened. Unforgiveness is terribly hard to detect in yourself.

There's an old saying that wisely reminds us: "The eye cannot see the eye." We need others to help us see our impure motives.

Lesson of the Leak

Some time ago, there was a leak in our office roof. One of the tiles was showing a growing wet spot. You might think we could simply remove that one tile, find the leak and take care of it. Not this leak. This leak was nowhere to be found!

After much effort (which seemed ridiculous and unnecessary) we finally located the leak. It had started way on the other side of the building. The dripping water had found a rafter and surfed that for a while. Then it found some wire and slid along that. Finally, at a sharp curve, the water lost its hold and started dripping, right above my office.

It was the most difficult thing to find the source of that leak. It was all the way across the building! But the damage turned up in my office, far over on the other side!

Unforgiveness is like that: It shows up in the most unexpected places, and finding its source is often difficult. For example, you might get angry with your cousin and allow unforgiveness to take root. That same lack of forgiveness shows up later in a relationship with someone that reminds you of your cousin. She may act nothing like your cousin, but she looks like your cousin or talks like her, and slowly but surely that unforgiveness sprouts up.

The same can be true if you have refused to forgive your parents. Years later, you could be halfway across the world, grown and married but you still have the same problems. That's how unforgiveness works: It is an *unresolved* issue. And like an open wound, unless you tend to it and heal it, it will always fester right below the surface.

A Real-Life Drip

Let me give you a real-life example. A particular woman was part of the leadership team at a church where I was involved. That was great, except that every time I suggested something at a meeting, she would always argue with me and then refuse to accept it. Every single time without fail. It didn't matter what I said; she would fight it.

I would try to appeal to her, "Now, wait a minute, that's a good idea!"

"Nope!" she would say, arms crossed and case closed. If I tried to offer a different solution, she would still find a bone to pick.

She got married a few years later, but sadly it soon ended in divorce. Nine years after that, I received a letter: "Dear Wayne, I need to ask for your forgiveness." She revealed that an uncle had molested her years before. An unforgiving spirit began to take root in her teen years, and years later, that unforgiveness flared up whenever a male authority figure appeared in her life. Because she had seen me as an authority figure, her lack of forgiveness spilled into our relationship. The leak that started over on the other side of her building showed up as an acid drip years later.

Unforgiveness bleeds into every area of your life and oozes out whenever pressure is applied. It stains your marriage, your family, your friendships, your leadership and your ministry. It is the nemesis to successful living.

Here's how one friend described it to our accountability group. For 10 years he held bitterness against his ex-wife after a contentious divorce. "Unforgiveness" he said, "was like a little vial of acid placed right behind my heart. Every time I moved, it spilled. The resentment would well up again. Each time I moved, it spilled, burning my heart again. It didn't even need to have anything to do with my current circumstance; it still spilled onto everything I cared about and ruined everything."

RESENTMENT: RE-FEELING THE PAIN

Unforgiveness eventually metastasizes into an enduring condition called "resentment."

Resentment stems from the Latin word *resento*. The two base words of that word are *re,* which means "again," and *sento,* which means "to feel the pain of a cut." It's not the actual cutting, but the *feeling* of the cut. Together these two words make up the word *resento,* which means "to feel the cut again." It allows you to feel pain over and over again.

Caution: Resentment always destroys the container that holds it much sooner than those upon whom it is poured. I like to say it this way: "Resentment is drinking poison and waiting for the other person to die."

An Unbelievable Fishing Story
Alex Pacheco, a New Hope pastor, was a fisherman for many years. One day, his largest fishhook, the one he

used for catching huge deep-sea ahi, grabbed his heel and dug in deep. He must have been standing near it when the winch pulled all the hooks out, flying up fast and catching him unaware. Not only had it hooked him, it was almost impossible to remove; the large hooks have a barb that releases on impact so that the hook won't slip out. This prevents the fish from getting away no matter how hard it struggles.

The pain was excruciating as the hook knifed right through the thick of his foot. Alex was forced to cut the line and turn home to get help. He radioed in and the closest medical attention he could find was a paramedic at a fire station. The medic agreed to meet him at the boat harbor as soon as he arrived.

When Alex arrived, his foot was already ballooning. Paramedics tried pulling the hook out, but the barb kept ripping his flesh. They tried cutting the wound open. No luck there, either. They finally realized the only way they would be able to get it out was to push the hook all the way through his foot, cut the tip, and then pull it back out. With a hesitant nod from Alex and a lot of prayer, they did it.

"Didn't that hurt worse?" I demanded when he told me the story. "Couldn't they have gotten it out any other way?"

Alex pondered and said, "They tried every way they could. And even though it hurt worse, one thing was clear: They were *not* going to leave it in!"

That's how we need to view unforgiveness: It *must* come out! Even if it causes more pain to get it out, it *cannot* be tolerated. If left in to fester, it will block God's plan for you.

Forgiving is the best plan for your physical health, by keeping the acid drip from infecting your insides with stress. It's also the best plan for emotional health, by keeping your relationships from souring. Mentally you will be freed of the resentment. And it's a plan for your spiritual health, to make sure you have the promising future God has planned for you. If we don't forgive, our lives will slowly but surely show the symptoms. Like Absalom, refusing to forgive will destroy every area of our lives: physical, mental, emotional and, most of all, spiritual.

When something happens—whether it's a perceived wrong or an actual wrong—if you don't forgive, it *will* imprison you in your past. A hurt acts like a very strong steel cord that anchors huge ships to the pier; it's necessary when you're at the dock to have that anchor to survive. If you were to set sail with that steel cord holding you fast, at first it would just slow you down. But if you still tried to sail on after that, the steel cord anchored to the dock would tear out a hunk of your ship. Even the mightiest of vessels cannot sail with a huge hole in the hull.

At first, hurt is a necessary response that helps us to survive in a healthy way—it alerts us that something wrong has happened in a current situation. However, if we don't release that hurt and resolve it in a healthy way, we will remain connected to the hurt. At first it will just slow you down, but ultimately it will rip out a chunk of you and hazard your very well-being!

Forgiveness is the only way to loose those mighty steel cords and free your heart from being torn and scarred. Do it quickly! It's a Rule that is necessary and vital to your life.

Some people object: "But you don't know what happened to me in the past! It's too hard to forgive! I can't get it out of my mind."

Prison of Pain

If this sounds like you, you're imprisoned by resentment, causing you to keep refreshing that hurtful event in your mind. It's *resento*, feeling the old cut again. The difference is, the hurt you feel now is self-inflicted. "I remember what he did to me, yeah, ooh, ouch, ow." The wound becomes fresh again and you can't get away from it. And until you forgive, you'll bring it up again and again . . . and again.

People sometimes tell me, "Wayne, I can't forget that!"

"Yes, you can," I reassure them. And at the same time I understand full well the difficulty of what I'm saying.

"How am I supposed to forget?" they ask.

My answer is, "You'll start forgetting when you stop bringing it up. Stop thinking about it; stop rehearsing it in your mind. You can forget because God forgets."

"God forgets?" they ask in utter shock.

"Absolutely!"

God Forgets

Through the prophet Jeremiah, the Lord said this about His forgiveness for His people: "I will forgive their iniquity, and their sin I will remember no more" (Jer. 31:34). Did you know that God intentionally forgets? That's because in God's eyes, your sin is forgotten when it's forgiven.

Forgiven means forgotten, plain and simple. This forgetting is not a result of old age, Alzheimer's, or dementia. It is purposeful and intentional. Rather than saying "forgetting," a better way of expressing it might be *not bringing it up*. He will never bring it up again. Ever. Once your sin is forgiven, it's as good as gone from God's point of view.

For some of us, it's hard to forget another's sin. We say, "Well, the memories are still there."

"Intentionally forget them," God tells us.

"That's denial!" we argue.

"No, it's not. It's a part of your inheritance," He reminds us. "I've given you the power to quit bringing it up and cutting yourself time and again. I've given you the ability to stop blaming your pain on that person."

Unforgiveness drains your life of the very best. It'll drain you of time, thought, energy, emotions . . . all of that adds up quickly and is costly! If you allow an acid drip to eat a hole in your soul, it will drain the best of your life today due to the rottenness of yesterday. Don't you dare!

The precious gift of forgiveness stops the acid drip and restores your life. What a gift! And it's not for the other person; it's for *you*! It restores God's promises and overflowing abundance to *you*.

SCENE 3: A FOOLHARDY FINALE

Let's return to the story of Absalom and take a look at the grand finale of his life. Absalom had succeeded in his campaign, amassing a strong following and staging a coup to kill his father and capture the throne.

David heard about this plot, and he and his entourage slipped out under the cloak of night, escaping the bitter wrath of his son. In the last-minute upheaval of his royal household, David told some of his wives and concubines, "Stay here because he's after me, not you. When it's all settled, we'll return to the palace." With that, the rest of his household made a run for it.

Absalom heard about the great escape and set his troops after them with a seek-and-destroy mission. Fortunately, they couldn't find the royal fugitives and returned to the City of David where Absalom took the throne, proclaimed himself king and banished his father. In an act of self-coronation and warped male dominancy, he set up a tent on the palace rooftop and sexually violated each of his father's wives.

In the margin of my Bible next to this lurid part of Absalom's story (2 Sam. 16:22), I wrote these words about unforgiveness: *It makes you become like the one you can't forgive.*

The most shocking part of Absalom's story is that he became the very man he hated. First he hated his half-brother, Amnon, for raping his sister. Then he hated his own father, King David, for banishing him. Yet as we tune back in to his story, we see that Absalom's refusal to forgive turned him into the very person he hated: a rapist and one who banished his own family.

The final, most hideous stage of unforgiveness is that it transforms you into the very person you can't forgive. It's a danger that threatens each of us. Maybe you have a supervisor you don't like. Your supervisor doesn't support you or speak well of you. You get mad and can't let it go. You end up telling someone, "I can't believe him. That's it! I'm going to give him a dose of his own medicine."

"Whoa! Wait a minute," your friend says. "Didn't you just say he speaks badly about you?"

"That's right!" you fire back.

"Then what are you doing right now?" your friend asks. "Aren't you speaking poorly about him? And," your friend continues, "you said he doesn't care about you . . . "

"That's right," you reply, "and I don't give a rip about him. I'm not going to support him either!"

Unforgiveness transforms you into the very one you can't forgive. You're exactly like him. The only difference is, you are blind to it. Because God understands this only too well, He warns us: "Let no one become like a bitter plant that grows up and causes many troubles with its poison" (Heb. 12:15, *TEV*).

God in My Car

I made this realization some time ago at the oddest time: driving in my car. Someone had wounded me pretty deeply, and he began to spread rumors about our church. We asked him not to do that but he continued. There was something he thought I should have done, and because I didn't, he came against me. I found out that he was warning people not to come to our church! Soon people stopped coming.

I thought, *What's going on?* I realized that like Absalom, this person was allowing his indignation to infect and poison others.

Soon afterward, I was driving and began to think about everything he had said. With each remembrance, I'd wince with pain again. The resentment mounted with each white line I passed. Line after line whizzed by, and memory after memory, until I was smoking with rage!

Ever have God show up in your car? He showed up in mine right then and said, "Wayne, you've become just like that man."

I thought, *No way! I'm nothing like him.*

But God said, "You are just like him. You're slandering him and sabotaging his reputation."

I still argued, presenting my case to God, "I'm not *doing* it. I'm just *thinking* it in my mind and my heart."

God brought to my mind a portion of Scripture: "Out of the heart comes evil thoughts and slanders and fornications and murders" (Matt. 15:19).

When I said these things about him in my heart, I was filling the inner chambers of my heart with ammunition. I was filling it with evil thoughts and slander, and one day it would come out and I would become just like him. "The mouth speaks out of that which fills the heart" (Matt. 12:14).

That revelation scared me. The Lord whispered to my heart, "You *must* forgive because forgiveness stops the mutating process that is going on right now."

That was a wake-up call for me.

Forgiveness has the ability to stop that degenerating process and restore God's best to your life. Your aim is not to become like your offender. Your heart's desire is to become like Jesus.

Let me ask you a key question: *Who do you need to forgive?*

It may take a phone call or a letter; it may be painful to talk to that person or to write it down. If there's no way to reach them, then you may have to deal with just forgiving them in your heart. Whatever it is, you *must* get the hook out because keeping it in is not an option.

Forgiveness: Letting God Be God

James 4:12 tells us, "There is only one Lawgiver and Judge, the One who is able to save and to destroy; but who are you who judge your neighbor?"

We know that God has said, "Vengeance is Mine. I will repay" (Rom. 12:19), but wouldn't it be great to be His extended hand? We all know that the wages of sin is death. The problem? *We* want to be the undertaker to make sure that death is delivered for the sin!

God will take care of the injustices in our lives if we let Him, and He will even turn it into good! But we must let Him do what only He can do. When I try to carry out what only God can do, I get crushed under the load. I cannot bear the burden of carrying out the sentence of sin. Only God can do that. And the only thing that can free me from that fatal tendency is forgiveness!

Absalom tried to be God and it killed him. His story ended tragically. King David finally returned to the city and one of his generals killed Absalom. That's a tragic finale, but it is the classic result of refusing to forgive. And Absalom is no different from any of us. Unforgiveness will kill us as well.

Your life doesn't need to have the same tragic ending. Forgiveness is God's gift that can rewrite a future destined for loneliness and barrenness. Forgiveness simply puts the consequences of sin in the hands of the true Judge. God is that Judge. Let Him do His assignment.

It will free us to do ours.

STAND BY YOUR CONVICTIONS

HEROD: SWAYED BY THE CROWD

The king said to the girl, "Ask me for anything you want, and I'll give it to you." And he promised her with an oath, "Whatever you ask I will give you, up to half my kingdom." She went out and said to her mother, "What shall I ask for?" "The head of John the Baptist," she answered.

MARK 6:22-24, *NIV*

Pop quiz time! Let's begin our lesson with a little quiz. Here are several scenarios that share a common element. What do all of these scenarios have in common? See if you can identify the theme:

1. An overachiever that everyone admires. Secretly he is still trying to outrun his father's haunting words: "You'll never amount to anything!"
2. A man like a reed in a rushing river. He goes with the flow and never speaks out or stands up for anything.
3. A teenage girl who thinks that sex and love are the same thing. She gives in to her boyfriend's urging, even though she doesn't really want to.
4. A woman who feels so insignificant that she blends into the background, a wallflower, always feeling left out and lonely.
5. A man who would never be accused of being a Christian at work because he never has the courage to talk about Jesus with his co-workers.

How did you do on your quiz? Time to mark our papers. Here's the answer: Each of these people is driven by a deep fear of rejection.

APPROVAL ADDICTS

The fear of rejection is a powerful force indeed. At every corner of our society, approval addicts can be found. And none of us is immune to approval's addictive lure.

We all occasionally wonder, "What do others think?" "Will they still like me?" or "How do I look?" But if these questions plague you, then you're living in a deadly trap: "The fear of man will prove to be a snare, but whoever trusts in the Lord is kept safe" (Prov. 29:25, *NIV*). This proverb tells us that when we fear men or their rejection, the trap has snapped on us.

Read between the lines and you'll see that addiction approval isn't new to our image-crazed society or modern media. Far from it! God wrote about it long ago because so many—great and small—suffer the same addiction.

An Addict's Edicts

King Herod was an absolute ruler of the Roman Empire, the feared overlord of Galilee, which is where Jesus lived. He built buildings bigger than anyone had ever seen, and palaces, and world-class cities like Tiberias. These were modern marvels of their day and are still toured today as amazing feats of architecture and power.

Herod was a man of great stature and accomplishment, yet he cowed to the crowd and gave way to their sway. Because he bit his nails reading opinion polls, he had John the Baptist axed and let Jesus be nailed.

Herod's life is a great example to us not because of his power but because of his fear. His weakness teaches us the indispensable wisdom that no matter how great one's position (or how low), none of us is immune to peer pressure.

It happened to another great king in the Old Testament, King Saul. Saul confessed that his addiction led to his downfall: "I sinned . . . I was afraid of the people so I gave in to them" (1 Sam. 13:11). No one is immune!

What is the source of approval addiction? How can we get caught up in the sway of the crowd? Three words: fear of rejection.

Fear of rejection almost always happens when you've been severely rejected by someone you were hoping to please. Maybe that rejection came from a schoolteacher, a member of the opposite sex, a sibling, or a parent. Or it may have even come from someone at church.

The scars of rejection may look healed as time goes on, but the reality is that they are just as raw today as when they were first inflicted. It's no use to be told, "Get over it!" Unresolved hurts can take root in your heart, causing a deep fear of ever being rejected again by anybody. When this powerful fear takes over, you'll see harmful effects.

WHAT FEAR OF REJECTION DOES TO US

It Allows Others to Manipulate Us

When you have a fear of rejection, you allow others to mold you into their expectations and desires. The fear of rejection often appears as a need to please, at any cost. Advertisers play on this need all the time: "Buy this product or you're an idiot! Everybody else is buying it; you may as well buy it, too." How many of us have bought something we didn't want, but we really didn't want to look dumb, so we bought it anyway? Sure, most of us have!

The first harmful effect that pops up from our fear of rejection is that we allow others to manipulate us. We do crazy things we would never have done otherwise. The fear of rejection doesn't stop there. It first allows others to manipulate us, and then . . .

It Causes Us to Conform to Peer Pressure

Isn't it true? We tend to walk like other people, talk like other people, act like other people, and dress like other people. Why? Because we don't want to be rejected. It's the overwhelming power of our deep-rooted fear! And when we conform to our peers, we are vulnerable to the third harmful effect of the fear of rejection:

It Keeps Us from Following the Truth

Why do you think some people don't tell the truth or "shave" the truth among their peers? Because they are afraid that if they speak the truth, people will reject them. Our fear has the power to keep us from speaking the truth, the whole truth and nothing but the truth. We crave approval above the need to speak truth. But that's not all . . .

It Prevents Us from Giving and Receiving Love

Unresolved past hurts can prevent future relationships. For example, if I was hurt or rejected by my family when I was a child, I might not risk getting involved in deep, meaningful relationships ever again. That's because I fear other people will reject me just as my family did.

Unfortunately, not taking risks means I might prevent myself from getting hurt, but I'm also cutting myself off from the only way I'll ever receive love: from others. I also prevent myself from the most necessary human function of all—giving love. I can neither receive nor give love, and end up very lonely indeed.

Mark Twain said it this way: "A cat that gets burned from sitting on a hot stove will not only *never* sit on a hot stove again, it won't sit on *any* stove after that." Sadly, fear of rejection can keep us from *any* meaningful relationship. And finally . . .

It Silences Our Sharing About Jesus Christ

Fear of rejection quiets us from speaking the greatest message we could ever hope to share. Sometimes we don't share our faith because we are more concerned about the approval of others than anything else in our lives. Scripture tells us this even happened when Jesus lived. Many believed about Jesus, but they would not admit it for fear of the Pharisees. They were more concerned to have the approval of men than the approval of God (see John 12:42-43).

Like Herod, these people sacrificed their relationship with Jesus for the approval of others. Shocking, right? Because these believers didn't share their faith, many others who could have been part of the Early Church were never given the opportunity. And we do exactly the same thing when we sacrifice our testimony because we're afraid of what others will think.

Look at those five terrible, long-lasting effects that the fear of rejection has on us:

1. We allow others to manipulate us.
2. We conform to peer pressure.
3. We don't follow the truth.
4. We prevent future relationships.
5. We keep silent rather than share the gospel.

Mind-blowing, isn't it? Yes, the fear of rejection really can affect every area of our life, just as it affected Herod's.

A Great Man, A Greater Weakness

Here's a ripe palace scandal: Just north of Galilee, Herod's domain, was an area known as Caesarea Philippi, where Herod's brother Philip was overseer. Philip was married to Herodias. At the time, Herod was still a very eligible, very rich and very powerful bachelor. Herod and Herodias hit it off, so she packed her bags, left Philip and moved in with his brother instead. The country was abuzz with the news.

John the Baptist heard the celebrity scandal. In his bachelor days, Herod had often listened to John's spin on life and appreciated the prophet's honesty and wise counsel. But Herod felt John overstepped his bounds when he said, "Wife-snatching is wrong. You can't steal your brother's wife just because you are king!"

Herodias decided she didn't like John and convinced her new love, Herod, to have him imprisoned.

And Herodias had a grudge against him and wanted to put him to death and could not do so; for Herod was afraid of John, knowing that he was a righteous and holy man, and kept him safe. And when he heard him, he was very perplexed; but he used to enjoy listening to him (Mark 6:19-20).

And a strategic day came when Herod on his birthday gave a banquet for his lords and military commanders and the leading men of Galilee [everybody he wanted to impress]; and when the daughter of Herodias herself came in and danced, she pleased Herod and his dinner guests; and the king said to the girl, "Ask me for whatever you want and I will give it to you." And he swore to her, "Whatever you ask of me, I will give it to you; up to half of my kingdom." And she went out and said to her mother, "What shall I ask for?" And she said, "The head of John the Baptist" (vv. 21-24).

A Regretful Promise

Although the king truly regretted his promise, he felt he had to keep it because he had made it in front of his distinguished guests. He immediately sent an executioner to bring back the head of John the Baptist, his friend.

Because of the sway of the crowd, King Herod violated his own conscience. He even went against the desires of his heart. He knew what was right and yet he violated it because he wanted to impress his guests. For the sake of their approval, he sacrificed a close advisor.

Every single one of us is susceptible to peer pressure. No matter what station you hold—whether you're a CEO, an employee, a student or a parent—we all have to make hard decisions at some point in life. Will you choose to please God or your peers?

At that moment our fear of rejection slams right into our fear of the Lord. The Bible says, "The fear of man is a snare, but those who trust in the Lord are safe" (Prov. 29:25). I would put it this way: "If you fear God, you will fear nothing else. If you fear man, you will fear everything else."

How do we overcome the powerful sway of the crowd? We all want to make the right choice, as hard as it may be. Let me share a few helpful ways to conquer the fear of rejection; that way, when you come to that critical decision, you'll come out strong!

PUT GOD IN FIRST PLACE

The most important step in overcoming peer pressure is to place God first. Why?

Because "the Lord is my light and salvation, I will fear no one" (Ps. 27:1, *TEV*). The Lord is described as *light* and *salvation*. Both are significant to understanding why we must place God first to overcome a fear of rejection.

God is described as *my light*. Light has several important purposes in our life. First, it *illuminates*. Light helps us to see things more clearly. The word "illumine" means "to bring understanding and insight." Most of us would agree that light is better than dark.

When I was in the eighth grade, my class took a field trip to the Oregon Caves. Plunging deep into the earth, the Oregon Caves are like sparkling cathedrals chiseled into the marble heart of the Siskiyou Mountains. Gripping handrails like real cave explorers, we teetered on a slender, rickety bridge, oohing and ahhing over the stalactite and stalagmite columns around us. Just then the guide said, "Okay, don't move for the next 10 seconds." She cut the lights. Blackness like soot was thrown into our eyes. We couldn't see a thing! But we could hear everything, every little thing, especially whimpers, cries, screams, and even one kid throwing up on the bridge. Finally the guide turned the lights back on. It's no fun being in complete darkness!

David said this same thing in his psalm: "When I am confused, God lights my way." Our heavenly Father would never leave us alone in the dark. He always uses His light to illuminate our way and, more important, to illuminate our life.

Second, light not only illuminates, but it also *protects*. Maybe you protect your house with light. Perhaps a motion-detector spotlight frightens intruders away. Whenever I watch a scary movie, I feel much better if every light in our house is on. Why? Am I being silly? Of course not! Light provides protection against things that may lurk in the dark.

Finally, light *energizes*. It naturally brightens up your mood just as it brightens up your day. If someone is depressed, a friend opens all of the curtains in the room, saying, "Let's get some light in here!" Why? Because light energizes; it lifts your mood. It gives energy to tackle the tasks of our days.

David said his relationship with God was like that. God helped him to see things more clearly so that he didn't have to be afraid. He gave David the security he needed and energized his life. When David placed God first as his life's light, he never fell prey to the sway of the crowd.

Do you have a relationship like that with God? Have you placed Him first, as the light of your life? If you haven't, you'll be susceptible to the fear of rejection and the sway of the crowd. Or maybe you're looking to someone else to be your light.

You Light Up My Life

Many song lyrics are about the fact that people find light in other people. Debby Boone sang, "You Light Up My Life." Stevie Wonder lit up the charts with, "You Are the Sunshine of My Life." You hear all these songs about light and life, but here's the problem: If other people are your light, you're in trouble! Why? Because other people burn out, wear out and die out. They're not reliable.

The Lord is the battery that will never die, the lamp that will never blow and the flame that will never be snuffed out. When we place God first, we know that He provides all the illumination, protection and energy we will ever need. And in that we'll overcome our natural fear of rejection. He is our All in All!

Understanding Salvation

The second half of Psalm 27:1 says, "the Lord is my . . . salvation, I will fear no one." What does salvation mean? David would answer that by saying, "No matter what happens, God will always love me." No matter what.

The Bible says, "[Nothing] will be able to separate us from the love of God" (Rom. 8:39). Jesus said it this way, "I will never desert you, nor will I ever forsake you" (Heb. 13:5). It doesn't matter if someone else rejects you, because God never will. He will *always* love you, *always* accept you, and *always* hold on to you.

One of the keys to confidence and self-esteem is not to psyche yourself up every morning or read self-help books. Simply understand how much God loves you. "Show me how much you love me, Lord. Then I can answer those who insult me" (Ps. 119:42, *TEV*). Knowing God's great love for you puts you beyond a shadow of a doubt.

Focusing on God's approval simplifies life. "For yourself, concentrate on winning God's approval" (2 Tim. 2:15, *Phillips*). Life zeroes out to one thing: "I will only do what pleases God." When I please Him, it's always the right thing to do. No matter what everybody else thinks, I have succeeded!

Nobody Likes Me

Have you ever realized that you can't please everybody? That not everyone likes you? If you have, then you've come to a wonderful place in life. That's life! You can't please all the people all of the time.

Even God can't please everybody! One group is praying, "Oh, God, turn the hurricane away from our islands!" While at the same time, another group is praying, "Bring it closer, Lord! It'll give us more surf!" One person prays for sunshine, another prays for rain. And if God can't please everybody, we'd be foolish to expect that we can.

Put God in first place and everything else will fall into place after that. Second, and some of you will *especially* like this one, is to put people in their place.

PUT PEOPLE IN THEIR PLACE

I can just hear some of you thinking, *I like that! Hallelujah, that's the first thing you've said, Wayne, that I've ever liked!*

Hold on! Before you throw a party, hear me through. I'm not saying to be rude, ungracious or discourteous.

I'm talking about putting others' *opinions* in their rightful place. That means having the right perspective and not overvaluing what people say.

First of all, don't assume that when other people pass judgment on you, their words are the infallible truth straight from God. Most likely, they're not! "The Lord says: 'I am the one who strengthens you. Why should you fear mortal man . . . ?'" (Ps. 27:1, *TEV*). Notice the word "mortal," which reminds us that what people say is temporary and soon passes away.

When others' opinions become all-important, you're setting yourself up for a big fall. You'll fall prey to the trappings of popularity, fame, applause, public opinion and "What will people think?" Image becomes everything.

From Hero to Zero

As the old song goes, some people say, "I wanna see my smilin' face on the cover of *Rolling Stone*." Well, even if fame does happen, you'll be a hero one day and a zero the next. Really, how many people who made the cover of *People* magazine two years ago are still riding high today? We don't even know where they are! They disappear after 15 seconds of fame; then what? First a hero, then a zero.

The apostle Paul told us exactly what he thought about living for man's approval:

Am I now trying to win the approval of man or of God? If I were still trying to please men, I would not be a servant of Christ (Gal. 1:10, *NIV*).

Paul said, "I have a choice: men or God. I choose God. Whatever I do will please Him."

Audience of One

One of the greatest ways we overcome the sway of the crowd is with every breath, every act, every thought: Always live for an audience of One. No matter what, live for God. It's His approval we want. The only One that matters.

But what about what others think? That is something you have to seriously consider. The answer to that would be, "If God is for us, who can be against us?" (Rom. 8:31, *NIV*). You see, when you realize how much God is for you, you'll be able to withstand tremendous rejection. Nothing in this world will be able to stand against you when you realize that God is for you and you are operating within His plan.

You might still wonder, "Can I ever stop caring about others' opinions?" Honestly, no. It's almost impossible not to be affected by them because we live with people. You would have to be without emotion (or dead!) to say, "I don't care what people think."

However, you can grow to a place in your life where you're no longer *directed* by others' opinions. You'll choose to be directed by God's plan, not others' expectations. Be forewarned: Some people will not like it, and they'll say the meanest things (especially well-meaning family members). It'll hurt! But don't let it direct you. Simply ask yourself, "Who am I trying to impress: others or God?" Answering this question will help you to put everything in the appropriate order; overcoming fear requires putting people in their place.

Finally, conquering your fear of rejection requires what may be the most difficult challenge of all three: putting *yourself* in your proper place.

PUT YOURSELF IN THE PROPER PLACE

Some people think more highly of themselves than they ought to think. Others think far too lowly of themselves. I would suggest that not many of us see ourselves with God's eyes. Very few of us realize how unique and how valuable we are to God. If we did, we would be able to withstand a lot of rejection.

Poor self-image is due to not understanding God's values, which is how we end up having a faulty value system. Although God values us highly, we don't. Then, when people criticize us, deep down we wonder if they're right.

Disabled Hearts

One of the ladies in our church was waiting for a bus when another lady from our church came and stood beside her at the stop. The second lady looked straight ahead, never acknowledging her friend.

The first lady started thinking, "She goes to my church but she's not even speaking to me! She probably doesn't like me. Well, if she doesn't talk to me, I'm not going to talk to her. And if she doesn't like me, then I don't like her either!"

The bus arrived and they both got on. About five minutes later, the second lady noticed the first and said, "Oh, Mabel! I'm so sorry, I didn't even see you!"

"Really?" said the first lady totally surprised at this turn of events.

"No! Please forgive me," she said, "I was so consumed in my thoughts that I didn't even see you. You see, I just came from the doctor and she informed me that my little boy has leukemia. I don't know what to do!"

Sometimes we're so involved in our own fears that we don't see the opportunities all around us to care for others. We only see our fear. And life starts to revolve around us. Soon we wonder what people think about me, mine and myself, and it's all about me!

The cure? Accept what God's Word says about you: "You (God) made man inferior only to Yourself. You crowned him with glory and honor" (Ps. 8:5, *TEV*). Isn't that wonderful? That means we're only inferior to God and no one else. We're all right up there, second to Him alone. Never allow yourself to feel inferior to others.

God Made Us *Great*!
You say, "But that's kind of a high place God's given us. I don't deserve that!" That's true. None of us really deserves that honor. However, Ephesians 1:4 says that through what Christ has done for us, God has decided to make us holy in His eyes. Without a single fault, we stand before God covered by His love, through what Christ has done.

We are acceptable to God, approved by God and loved by God. Not because of our own merit or because of what we've done. You will never be good enough to please a perfect God based on your own accomplishments. It's only through what Jesus Christ did that we have been made acceptable.

So it doesn't matter what you say about yourself. Sometimes I don't think I deserve God's approval. The Lord says, "I understand that, but you know what really counts, Wayne? *It's what I say about you*." What makes us acceptable is what God says and what Jesus did, and we get to rest in that. "It is not self-commendation that matters, it is winning the approval of God" (2 Cor. 10:18, *TEV*).

Sway of the Crowd or Way of the Lord?

Simplify your life by saying, "I will only do what pleases God." It's a vital Rule to living successfully. When you put God in first place, others in their place, and yourself in the right place, you'll have a confidence that cannot be shaken. You'll see a world of great promise coming to pass for your life—the promises of the Living God coming true in you!

MAINTAIN HEALTHY RELATIONSHIPS

ABIGAIL: APPEASING THE KING

When Abigail saw David, she quickly got off her donkey and bowed down before David with her face to the ground. She fell at his feet and said: "My lord, let the blame be on me alone. Please let your servant speak to you; hear what your servant has to say."

1 SAMUEL 25:23-24, *NIV*

Imagine if you could have *anything* you desired. Wouldn't that be a dream come true? Nothing could make you happier!

Ever dream of owning a $700,000 Ferrari Enzo? How about two? What about a mansion with a pool? Throw in a few motorcycles, jet skis and acres upon acres of land. In fact, make it your own private island! A yacht? Of course! For spending money, how about a neat 50 million?

Happy?

Only one catch: You get to live the rest of your life on that island . . . alone. No contact with anyone else.

Still happy?

Life loses its luster unless you have someone to share it with, doesn't it? You can have the best of the best, but if there is no one to enjoy it with, brag to, impress, or laugh with, what use is it?

In the absence of others, even the best of us goes crazy. The worst torture known to man is just that: solitary confinement. It could be set in plush, five-star surroundings, but it would still be torture!

God's Design

God never intended for us to live alone. We function only in relationship with others. Without healthy relationships, nothing else really matters. God designed it that way, and unless we get this next Rule of Success down cold, life will always hold us accountable for a missing piece: the absence of healthy relationships.

One woman in the Bible teaches us this most valuable lesson: An indispensable ingredient of life is healthy relationships. Abigail married a man who was a simple sheepherder, but his gradual success morphed him into someone else. The ruse of his riches gave rise to his lack of character. Her story unfolds in the book of 1 Samuel:

> The man's name was Nabal, and his wife's name was Abigail. [She] was intelligent and beautiful in appearance, but the man was harsh and evil (1 Sam. 25:3).

In that day, flocks reflected how wealthy you were, and Nabal was rich! He had 3,000 sheep and 1,000 goats. He lived in the wilderness with thousands of sheep and goats, and no showers . . . which means he wasn't just rich; he was stinking rich!

But his true downfall?

He was also stinking selfish!

Sharing the Desert

Living in the same desert was young David, a fugitive on the run from a raging madman. King Saul feared this talented young man would soon inherit his throne, so he became obsessed with preventing that from happening, at any cost!

Sharing the desert with Nabal were others of a shadier type—thieves and sand pirates—who reveled in pillaging unguarded sheepherders. On several occasions, David and his men drove off the scavengers to protect Nabal's herds.

At that time, the annual sheep-shearing days were a celebration everyone looked forward to; it was the Old Testament equivalent of a carnival, or a "Desert County Fair." It was a gala event commemorating the profits of local land barons like Nabal.

Any Take Out?

At this party, David sent 10 men to ask for leftover food. He expected Nabal to be overjoyed to share his bounty with his volunteer sheriffs. However, instead of gratefulness, Nabal sent a helping of hot humiliation: He sent David's men back not with food, but with half-shaven beards.

One thing you just don't do is disgrace a desert militia commanded by a giant-slayer. David immediately declared war on Nabal, ready to balance the scales. "In vain have we been protecting this selfish egotist," David declared. "By this time tomorrow, none of his men will be alive!" They mounted up and headed for the fairgrounds.

A Woman vs. an Army

When Nabal's wife heard of the impending massacre, she knew that unless she intervened, it would be more than sheep sheered at this party. She had to repair a devastated relationship . . . and *fast!*

> Then Abigail hurried and took two hundred loaves of bread and two jugs of wine and five sheep already prepared and five measures of roasted grain and a hundred clusters of raisins and two hundred cakes of figs, and loaded them on donkeys . . . When Abigail saw David, she hurried and dismounted from her donkey, and fell on her face before David and . . . said, "On me alone, my lord, be the blame" (1 Sam. 25:18-19,23-24).

Abigail's quick intervention impressed David, and her humility softened his warrior heart. She had answered for the foolishness of her husband.

Then David said to Abigail, "Blessed be the LORD
God of Israel, who sent you this day to meet me,
and blessed be your discernment . . . Unless you
had come quickly to meet me, surely there would
not have been left to Nabal until the morning
light as much as one male . . . Go up to your
house in peace. See, I have listened to you and
granted your request" (1 Sam. 25:32, 34-35).

Abigail knew that leaving a burnt bridge in disre-
pair would result in devastating consequences. Always
remember: A life of faith is built on *action*. A life of fear
is built on *avoidance of action*!

Abigail understood faith!

Thanks to quick thinking *and* action, she was able
to save the day. From this wise woman, we can learn an
indispensable Rule of Success about how to repair broken relationships.

TAKING AND HOLDING OFFENSES

Some years ago, I was in a local restaurant when a middle-
aged gentleman slid into the booth opposite me. "You're
Wayne Cordeiro, aren't you?" He said with urgent tones.
"I need help. I'm a pastor and our church has flat-lined

for some years now. Do you have anything to bring it back to life? A new book? A magazine? A DVD?"

I chuckled and asked him to give me some background; who was he and where was he from?

"Well," he sighed, bracing himself, "as I said, I'm the new pastor. This is my second year, but I was an assistant before that."

"How was the church when you took it two years ago?" I asked.

"Terrible! I don't think I should say anything more than that!"

I gently coaxed, "Now tell me what went wrong."

He embarked on a story that I will never forget, recalling the day he received the leadership baton: "It was a Sunday morning. There must have been a hundred in attendance, and something in the air was foreboding. After a few hymns, the pastor got up and in a monotone drone said, 'Could I have the board members stand?'

"After a moment of shuffling, a half-dozen or so men stood to their feet. From the pulpit, the pastor continued, 'It's because of these men that I am now leaving the church.' With that he picked up his Bible and left! And that's how I became the pastor."

I was dumbfounded. "No way!" I said disbelievingly. "That did *not* happen that morning!"

"Oh, yes it did," he replied. "I was there!"

"But it didn't happen that morning," I repeated, more firmly.

"What do you mean?" he pressed.

"It may have surfaced that morning, but it didn't *happen* that morning. It began a year or two before when people began to tolerate broken relationships and burying unresolved anger with one another."

What's Most Important

I gave my best counsel: "Here's your new program: Start no new programs! At least for 12 months. Instead, go to each person, look them in the eye and ask, 'Are we doing okay?' Make sure there are no hidden hurts, no unresolved offenses, no smoldering bridges that need to be rebuilt. Start with those closest to you, and work your way outward until no one has any unsettled accounts. If not, consider canceling church until all is progressing smoothly."

By his countenance, I could tell that this new friend had now turned into a foe. He rebuked me: "Who do you think you are to make such a demand?"

I apologized, "I'm sorry. Did I lead you to believe that I was the one that said that? Actually, I need to credit the original source, Jesus. In Matthew 5:23 and 24,

He said: 'If you are presenting your offering at the altar, and there remember that your brother has something against you, leave your offering there before the altar and go; first be reconciled to your brother, and then come and present your offering.' In other words, having right relationships is more important than just attending church!"

Healthy Bodies

What takes place in families and in churches is mirrored in our own bodies. If we are basically healthy and fundamentally sound, we will rarely get sick. If we do become ill, it's not long before we are back on our feet. However, if our bodies are filled with anxieties, suspicions, unresolved guilt and unsettled stresses, we will be found susceptible to every virus that floats within a mile of us. When we do get sick, we will stay sick for a long time. Our resiliency fades and is replaced with a vulnerability to passing illnesses.

Churches, families and relationships are *living entities*, in much the same way that human bodies are living entities. The existence of a low-grade discontent and the presence of unresolved offenses will impair the health of individuals and relationships. Nothing can move forward until anger is diffused and offenses are remedied.

God can't start the healing process until we reprioritize healthy relationships.

Nullifying God Himself

We find a startling discovery in Mark 6 about living with unresolved offenses. Jesus is in His hometown of Nazareth, where He's asked to address the synagogue. As He concludes, the critics begin their pitiful diatribes:

> "Is not this the carpenter, the son of Mary, and brother of James and Joseph and Judas and Simon? Are not His sisters here with us?" And they took offense at Him . . . And He could do no miracle there (Mark 6:3,5).

Naysayers were mixed in with the onlookers. They took offense and seized the opportunity to discredit the young prophet. The result?

"And He could do no miracle there."

No, it doesn't say that He "would" do no miracle. It specifically states that He *could* do no miracle, due to their offense. We nullify the power of God to heal by displacing it with offense. If we take offense, we lose the miraculous.

Jesus called it *unbelief.*

Refusing to Be Offended

We all have dozens of opportunities in the rush of daily life to be offended:

- You are passed over for a promotion.
- You are not consulted on something you felt you should have had input on.
- You are not invited to a luncheon.
- You are not called on your birthday by a loved one.
- You are not thanked appropriately for a deed you did.
- Your pastor didn't visit you when you were in the hospital.

Each of us will have occasion to take offense, retaining an insult due to a misdemeanor. But if there was ever anyone who had the "right" to be offended, it would have to be Jesus. He was slandered, betrayed, pursued, hated, lied about, and ultimately beaten, falsely accused, and crucified. Yet on the cross He said, "Father, forgive them; for they do not know what they are doing" (Luke 23:34).

In foretelling the Messiah, Isaiah described Him in these terms: "He will not be disheartened or crushed until

He has established justice in the earth" (42:4). Does this mean Jesus would never have any opportunity to be disheartened? No! Instead, it is written, "He *will not* be disheartened." He simply refused! As Messiah, Jesus refused offense. Why?

He knew about the great miracle of redemption that was needed.

What Destroys God's People

Think of it this way: Offenses are the sins of others. "Taking offense" means that we willingly capture the other person's offense and hold on to it.

Sin passes through our lives all the time. If we let it come and go, we will be unaffected. On the other hand, if we "take offense," we are *choosing* to hold on to it. Holding on to offense will impede you from positioning your life for the miraculous.

> He said to them, "Receive the Holy Spirit. If you forgive the sins of any, their sins have been forgiven them; if you retain the sins of any, they have been retained" (John 20:22-23).

If you retain sin, whether yours or another's, then heaven says those sins will be retained. On the other hand, if you forgive sins, they will be forgiven! Taking offense clouds the atmosphere for the miraculous and hinders God's ability to bestow His grace.

THE CASE OF UNRESOLVED SIN

There are three ways we can retain sin and thereby destroy relationships. One case is obvious, but in the other two cases, we may not even realize we're doing it. The first case is pretty clear:

When I Am Wrong

When I am wrong and I commit a sin, a spiritual debt is incurred. Sin is a taskmaster that demands its wages to be paid in full. Psalm 32 says, "When I was silent about my sin, my body wasted away as with the feverish heat of summer. For thy hand was heavy upon me." It manifests itself in physical symptoms and relational consequences. According to Romans 6:23, the consequence of sin is death, perhaps not physical, but a death in relationships, marriages, families and churches.

On the other hand, through the biblical principle of repentance, the debt of sin is satisfied. Resolving it allows for the miraculous. Once that happens, healing and restoration can begin.

The next scenario in which we might retain sin is more dangerous because it is more difficult to recognize . . .

When I Am Right

We are most vulnerable to being wrong *when we are right*. Let me explain: When we are right, we feel justified in attacking others. We use our "rightness" (or *self-righteousness*) to endorse our contention. After all, we're right!

When you are on the "wrong" side of the cross, it's humbling. When you are on the "right" side of the cross, it's dangerous! Often I have seen people use rightness as a whipping post or as a podium to denounce others, all in the name of being right!

Stewarding "rightness" is a difficult assignment. Remember, Jesus was right, even sinless, but when He was on the cross, His rightness did not cause Him to condemn those who were responsible for the injustice. Instead, Jesus begged forgiveness for His offenders. He knew that the redemption of mankind was at stake, and He traded in His right to feel offended for the sake of our redemption. Stewarding rightness is an unnerving mission, but doing so will nurture an atmosphere of the miraculous and bring about wholeness and redemption.

MAINTAINING HEALTHY RELATIONSHIPS

Winning at life means having great relationships. And having a great relationship requires a strict regimen of nurturing those relationships. Fruitful relationships require high maintenance!

It is somewhat in vogue to have silk plants in our homes. They require no watering, only periodic dusting. Real ones demand fertilization, sunlight, appropriate watering and a watchful eye for bugs! We have some in our home. (Not bugs, mind you, but silk plants.) We have a fig tree, some flowers, even an apple sapling. They do brighten the interior of our home, but there are two major disadvantages: Fake plants don't emit the fragrance that real ones do, and they can never bear fruit!

Relationships are like that, too. If we want fruitful ones, ones that are refreshingly fragrant, then they will require maintenance! It is one of life's success secrets. Here are three ways to maintain a healthy relationship, whether it is a friendship, your marriage or your family:

GO FIRST

God's Word gives us a good starting block: Healthy relationships always begin with ourselves! "A man who has friends must himself be friendly" (Prov. 18:24, *NKJV*).

Sometimes I think good relationships should begin with my kids straightening up, or with my wife getting some therapy. But the Bible says they must begin with me! I must be the one who is watering and nourishing the relationships around me.

When it comes to nurturing relationships, a crucial Rule of Success is: Go first!

I once stood in a busy coffee shop and watched the grumpy people stand in line for their drug of choice, caffeine. No one talked and no one smiled. It resembled a condolence line in a funeral parlor, with people waiting to pay their respects.

I decided to try an experiment. Instead of waiting for them, I thought I would initiate a greeting and see how people would respond. Although they resembled criminals on death row, I thought it would be fun giving it a try.

So I turned to the first person and with a smile, I said cheerfully, "Good morning!"

That person brightened and responded, "Good morning!" It was like a miracle of resurrection had just taken place; that which was once dead had come to life.

Then I tried it with several other people; 100 percent of the comatose coffee shop patrons responded with life! So I tried it at home, where the response was the same. Regardless of how things seem, a cheerful word and a positive blessing has a powerful effect.

Abigail must have known that. When Nabal lit David's fuse, Abigail took the initiative. She found David on his way to execute a death sentence, and intercepted. "Good morning, David!" she said cheerfully.

"What's so good about it? I'm on my way to finish some business! Move aside."

Go First in Diffusing Anger

Abigail knew that she needed to diffuse his anger, so she took the initiative to go first: "She fell at his feet and said, 'On me alone, my lord, be the blame'" (1 Sam. 25:24). A powerful life principle is accepting blame to rebuild a broken relationship. Who is truly at fault is not the issue. Abigail was innocent, but she understood that for healing to begin, anger had to be diffused.

Jesus did that for us. His death on the cross was the beginning of our healing and forgiveness. It inaugurated redemption for the world.

My wife, Anna, is a picture to me of the Abigail Principle. Regardless of who is at fault, she will often go first in taking the blame (although as a husband, it should be me!). But when she does, anger is diffused and repair begins.

This principle moves us from the problem side of the equation to the solution side. Taking the blame doesn't mean Anna is guilty. Rather, she initiates the diffusing of anger so that healing can begin. She is more committed to finding health in our relationship than she is to finding who is at fault.

Go First in Speaking Words That Heal

With the anger diffused, Abigail encouraged the rebuilding process:

> Please forgive the transgression of your maidservant; for the Lord will certainly make for my lord an enduring house, because my lord is fighting the battles of the LORD, and evil will not be found in you all your days (1 Sam. 25:28).

Our conversation isn't always uplifting; in fact, sometimes it's a doomsday commentary, a litany of curses, and a repetition of discouragement:

- "It's useless."
- "Our marriage is over."
- "I've got nothing left."
- "We'll never get out of debt."

- "We've tried everything. Nothing works."
- "He'll never change."
- "She'll never change."
- "I can't change. That's just the way I am!"

Dead-end words. We repeat them with religious fervor, and by doing so, we become undone!

Abigail teaches us how to nurture healthy relationships before they die, by reminding us that words carry great power to either kill or bring life. Words can turn a healthy relationship sour or a soured relationship back to health.

The story is told of a woman so intent on divorcing her husband that she hired the vilest lawyer she could afford. "I don't want to just divorce him," she said, "I want to *devastate* him!"

The devious lawyer pondered for a moment, and then he laid out his plot: "Let's take him by such surprise. Make him so shocked and overwhelmed . . . "

"I like that!" said the soon-to-be ex-wife. "How do we do that?"

"For three months," sneered the lawyer, "build him up like you've never done before. Speak words that make him feel like a million bucks. Do it every day, day in and day out. Then, when we hand him the divorce papers, he'll be so shocked! And we'll easily take him for all he has!"

Well that's just what the woman wanted, the perfect payback.

That evening, her plan unfolded. Inspiring words, encouraging responses, and kind answers flowed from her every tone, every word and every nuance . . . all the necessary ingredients to concoct a deadly potion that he would drink to the full.

He was caught in her cunning web, one that spun until the day of his final execution.

As the three-month deadline drew near, she met with her lawyer. "Are you ready to sign the divorce papers?" he said with a gleam in his eye. "We'll have the sheriff deliver them! Oh, how I would love to see his face. Ready to sign?" He was quivering with anticipation.

"Sign?" the woman replied. "I can't sign those papers! Why in the last three months, he's become the nicest man I have ever met!"

Go First in Doing Good

Romans 12:21 instructs us in another life principle: "Do not be overcome by evil, but overcome evil with good."

Being silent or being neutral does not overcome evil; evil can only be reversed by an action of goodness.

It is repealed by an act of kindness. It is annulled by unexpected gift-giving.

Abigail knew that. She diffused David's anger, encouraging him instead: "And now let this gift which your maidservant has brought to my lord be given to the young men who accompany my lord" (1 Sam. 1:25-27).

Our normal reaction when things are going bad is to start to withhold and draw back. We cease giving gifts of encouragement. We stop taking time to listen. We no longer overlook the idiosyncrasies of another. We discontinue notes of appreciation, abandon the smiles and lose the laughter. Love covers a multitude of sins but we draw back the covers!

And we justify our withholding:

- "She doesn't deserve a favor."
- "He doesn't merit my patience."
- "My coworker doesn't warrant a thank-you note. After all, it's his job!"

A powerful Rule of Success is gift-giving. Why? Because it impedes the intrusion of evil, inhibits the erosion of life, and initiates fruitfulness. But the test of gift-giving is not when things are going well. Gift-giving is best applied as a catalyst for healing when things are *not* going well!

COLLECTING FRIENDS

As a young upstart pastor, one of my dearest friends was Noel Campbell. He is in his golden years now, but he was a mentor to me while I cut my teeth.

At that time, "Pog" collecting was the rage. Pogs are wax-milk bottlecaps usually inscribed with the dairy's moniker. Everyone prophesied that Pogs would out-do baseball cards as collectibles, and I traded, bartered, swapped, negotiated and haggled to get the best of them.

Satisfied with my stash, I showed Noel my fine collection. Then I said, "Noel, some collect baseball cards, and others collect Pogs. What are you collecting?" Noel's wise reply took me off guard:

"I collect friends."

I have been to hundreds of funerals, and never have I heard anyone say of the dearly departed, "What I appreciated most about Harry was his money!" No, in the end we hear what was most enduring: "What I loved most about Harry was that he took the time to listen. He was a good friend!"

In the end, we will only have relationships; they are the only things that will last. When the curtains draw to a close, relationships will be the most valuable. So why wait? It's a Rule of Success that will inspire success: maintaining healthy relationships.

Awaiting God's Best

Life is lived best by the Book, and when you honor its laws, you will soar higher than you ever dreamed possible. However, there are no guarantees for smooth landings. We will all face speed bumps and even a few setbacks, but when you keep your eyes on the Giver of Life, *you will make it*!

The life of the godly is not a nicely paved, straight interstate highway; it's more like a back road. The back road through the Blue Ridge Mountains of Tennessee is a great example: There are blind curves and hairpin turns that send you backward in order to go forward. All along this hazardous, twisted road that doesn't let you see very far ahead, are frequent signs that say, "The best is yet to come."

This book was designed to be one of those signs to give you some hope, to remind you that all the perplexing turns in your life are not dead-end streets, and to encourage you because when you follow God's Rules of Success, you can be assured of one thing . . . The best is yet to come!